ORIOLES
ESSENTIAL

ORIOLES
ESSENTIAL

Everything You Need to Know
to Be a Real Fan!

Thom Loverro

TRIUMPH
BOOKS

Library of Congress Cataloging-in-Publication Data

Loverro, Thom.
  Orioles essential : everything you need to know to be a real fan! / Thom Loverro.
    p. cm.
  Includes bibliographical references.
  ISBN-13: 978-1-57243-832-3 (hard cover)
  ISBN-10: 1-57243-832-0 (hard cover)
   1. Baltimore Orioles (Baseball team)—Miscellanea. 2. Baseball fans—United States—History [1. Baltimore Orioles (Baseball team)—History]. I. Title.

GV875.B2L67 2007
796.357'64097526—dc22

                                                        2006030306

This book is available in quantity at special discounts for your group or organization. For further information, contact:

Triumph Books
542 South Dearborn Street
Suite 750
Chicago, Illinois 60605
(312) 939-3330
Fax (312) 663-3557

Printed in U.S.A.
ISBN: 978-1-57243-832-3
Design by Patricia Frey
All photos courtesy of AP/Wide World Photos except where otherwise indicated

Contents

Foreword

Baltimore is very much a blue-collar town. People here seem to appreciate the hard work that takes place on the field. I had a lot of fans in Baltimore, and I think the main reason for that was I went out there every time I was asked to and played as hard as I could. There wasn't a day that I came to the ballpark and didn't give my best. People in Baltimore seem to appreciate that type of approach. The guys from the glory years of Orioles baseball—from Frank Robinson to Brooks Robinson to Boog Powell to Dave McNally—even though they were some of the biggest names in baseball at the time, they went out there and gave it everything they had every day.

And later on, in another generation, you have to look at guys like Cal Ripken Jr. and Eddie Murray. Those were two names that a manager could write into the lineup comfortably every single day. Eddie is the guy Cal often praises for showing him the right way to approach the game. Eddie played 160 games or more every single year. He might have taken a day off occasionally, but he truly was an everyday player. Guys like Eddie and Cal, two superstar-caliber players who came to the ballpark ready to play day in and day out for years, are great examples of the stability that came to symbolize the Orioles organization.

That stability was also evident in the way the game was taught at all levels of the organization. If Dad [Cal Ripken Sr.] called for a bunt play at the Double A level and Rich Dauer executed the play, he might find himself in a big-league uniform a week later being asked to execute the exact same bunt play by manager Earl Weaver. Things were done the same way at every level, so when the players reached the big leagues they all knew exactly what was expected of them.

There was stability there. There was a system in place coordinated by people who were able to communicate a consistent message. They didn't go off course. That is the way it was done—"the Oriole Way." That is the way we did things throughout the organization, and in my mind that is the reason why the franchise was baseball's most consistent over a 30-year period.

Baltimore fans like knowing their team. They like to know who is going to be on the field and enjoy developing an almost-personal relationship with each player. It's not that easy for fans to do that anymore. Every year there are a lot of new names on the roster. It wasn't that way just a few years back. You could count on Brooks playing third and Boog playing first and McNally taking the hill. And even though Cal played with a lot of different second basemen and third basemen next to him, there was always that stability when he and Eddie were together in the middle of the lineup. And every fan knew it. Orioles fans understood that they could walk up to Memorial Stadium, buy a ticket, and watch Cal and Eddie terrorize opposing pitchers. On top of that, players such as Scott MacGregor, Mike Flanagan, and Jim Palmer anchored the pitching staff for a long, long time.

I think the fans of Baltimore really enjoyed the stability of the franchise and the familiarity that they developed with the players. The Oriole Way was evident every time the team took the field, and because it was an approach that proved to be successful for such a long time, the fans really fell in love with the team's makeup and style of play. They made a strong, positive connection with Frank, Brooks, Palmer, and so on. Orioles teams went out there and gave it everything they had without taking a day off. Just like the people of Baltimore. That is why this town fell in love with baseball, and why so many of the former players are still revered here. The connections that were made in years past still hold up today, because that was the Oriole Way—for both the players and the fans.

—Bill Ripken

Welcome to Baltimore

Baltimore baseball fans would welcome their new team in style for the 1954 season with a grand Opening Day parade on April 15. There may have been high expectations, since this team went 18–12 during spring training in Yuma, Arizona—the best record of all major league clubs. But while they were dressed up in new uniforms in a new city with a new name, these were still the St. Louis Browns, a woeful last-place team.

Jimmy Dykes would be the Orioles' first manager. Born in Philadelphia, Dykes was a longtime baseball man who made a reputation for himself over 15 seasons with the Philadelphia Athletics as a hard-nosed competitor who could play nearly any position. His manager, the legendary Connie Mack, once said, "Having one Dykes is like having five or six players and only one to feed, clothe, and pay."

He was an integral part of those great Athletics teams of the late 1920s—spending much of his time at third base—and was traded in September 1932, along with Al Simmons and Mule Haas, to the White Sox for $100,000. Two years later, Dykes took over as White Sox manager, serving as player-manager until 1939, and stayed until early in 1946. He had a reputation for being one of the most brutal bench jockeys in the game. Dykes joined the Athletics as a coach in 1949 and then was named manager in 1949. He did not have success back home and was fired, which made him available to manage the Orioles in 1954.

Dykes's roster included pitchers Don Larsen and Bullet Bob Turley, both future Yankees, and Vern Stephens and Vic Wertz—major league players in a minor league city with major league hopes and dreams. And those dreams were not dashed by the start of the

1

1954 Orioles

Pitchers
Vern Bickford
Mike Blyzka
Bob Chakales
Joe Coleman
Ryne Duren
Howie Fox
Jay Heard
Dave Koslo
Lou Kretlow
Bob Kuzava
Don Larsen
Dick Littlefield
Billy O'Dell
Duane Pillette
Marlin Stuart
Bob Turley

Catchers
Clint Courtney
Les Moss
Ray Murray

Infielders
Connie Berry
Jim Brideweser
Chico Garcia
Billy Hunter
Frank Kellert
Bob Kennedy
Dick Kryhoski
Vern Stephens
Eddie Waitkus
Bobby Young

Outfielders
Cal Abrams
Gil Coan
Chuck Diering
Joe Durham
Jim Fridley
Dick Kokos
Don Lenhardt
Sam Mele
Vic Wertz

season, opening on the road against the Detroit Tigers, splitting a two-game series, with the Orioles' first franchise win coming on April 14, a 3–2 victory over the Tigers. Duane Pillette was the club's first winning pitcher.

The Orioles came home for Opening Day on April 15 at Memorial Stadium and Baltimore's new Major League Baseball team posted a 3–1 win by Turley over the White Sox. Stephens and Clint Courtney both hit home runs off Chicago starter Virgil Trucks. Vice President Richard M. Nixon threw out the first pitch.

One week later, on April 21, the first night game was played at Memorial Stadium, with 43,000 fans watching Turley strike out a club-record 14 batters in a 2–1 loss to the Cleveland Indians. Turley had a no-hitter with one out in the top of the ninth inning when Al Rosen singled and Larry Doby slammed a two-run home run for the win. Two days later Baltimore won its first extra-inning game, when Ray Murray drove home two runs with a tenth-inning double to beat the White Sox 3–1 in Chicago. Two days after that, the club played its first doubleheader in Chicago and lost both games, 4–3 and 3–2. One month later on May 16, they played a doubleheader at Memorial Stadium before the largest crowd (46,796) that would see an Orioles game in the first 10 years the franchise was in Baltimore. The hometown lost the first game to the Yankees but came back to win the second game 6–2, with Larsen getting the win. Orioles fans saw a real treat that day, because there weren't many games Larsen would win in that 1954 season.

The Orioles went on to match the Browns' record in their last season in St. Louis, going 54–100. Don Larsen had a 3–21 record, and those 21 losses still remain the franchise record. Vic Wertz hit just .202 in 29 games and was traded during the season to the Cleveland Indians, where he went on to hit 14 home runs, drive in 48 runs, and help the Indians win a record 111 games and the American League pennant that year—57 games ahead of the seventh-place Orioles. Given that record, Turley had a remarkable season, posting a 14–15 record. He led the league in both walks and strikeouts. In a July 3 game against the Tigers at Memorial Stadium, Turley walked nine batters, but won the game 5–3 when Stephens hit an inside-the-park home run. He was the Orioles' stopper, at one point putting an end to a 14-game losing streak with a 5–3 win over Boston on August 26.

Besides Opening Day, the other high point of the season was a 10–0 win over the defending World Champion New York Yankees on July 30. Ironically, even though Larsen had just three wins, this one came against the team with which two years later he would make baseball history by pitching the only perfect game in World Series history.

There was another player on that 1954 roster who had a moment in not just baseball history, but literary history as well—Eddie

Waitkus. He was the talented first baseman who, while playing for the Phillies in 1949, was shot in the chest and almost killed by a young woman he did not know in a Chicago hotel room. That incident was the real-life inspiration for Bernard Malamud's *The Natural.*

There was one other noteworthy name on the roster of that inaugural 1954 Orioles team—a 5'7", 150-pound left-handed pitcher named Jehosie Heard, the first black player for the Baltimore Orioles. Heard had signed with the Browns in 1951, and pitched for a Western International League Class A team in Victoria, British Columbia, going 20–12. He was promoted to the Class AAA Portland club in 1953, where he went 16–12, and his contract was purchased by the Orioles after the Browns moved to Baltimore.

Satchel Paige, who had pitched for the Browns in 1953, could have been the first black player for the Orioles. But club officials

Orioles shortstop Billy Hunter is forced out at home by Yankees catcher Yogi Berra in this action shot from the Birds' first season in 1954. The Orioles lost 100 games that year but managed to avoid the cellar.

released him, saying he was too old and cost too much money. So Heard made the Opening Day roster, and was the only African American on the team that rode in the parade through the city.

TRIVIA

Who led the 1954 Orioles in wins?

Answers to the trivia questions are on pages 165–166.

Heard made his debut on April 24 in an afternoon game against the Chicago White Sox at Comiskey Park. With the Orioles trailing 10–0, he came on in relief with two outs in the bottom of the sixth inning. He faced four batters and retired them all. Baltimore lost 14–4. Heard would make just one other appearance that year, and he never played for the Orioles again.

Later that season, the Orioles called up another black player, outfielder Joe Durham, who became the first African American Oriole to hit a home run in September 1954. The Orioles actually finished that month with a winning record, going 11–10, and wound up drawing 1,060,910 fans (at the time, the most of any last-place club in baseball history) that first year in spacious Memorial Stadium— Death Valley for home run hitters. A total of 43 home runs were hit in the ballpark that season by both the Orioles and the visiting clubs, with Baltimore hitters accounting for 19 of them.

The rookie owners were ill-equipped in the ways of the business of baseball, and their record reflected it. So did some of the trades they made. Before the start of the season, the front office dealt away Roy Sievers, who become an outstanding power hitter (235 home runs over the next eight seasons), to the Washington Senators for Gil Coan, who turned in two lackluster seasons in Baltimore before being traded to the White Sox for the waiver price in 1955.

Dykes told reporters a story about his relationship with team president Clarence Miles:

"When I became manager of the Orioles in 1954, we had a president who said he knew nothing about baseball, and he couldn't have made a truer statement. But as the season went along, he thought he was becoming an expert at the game. Before long, he was saying, 'Dykes, do this,' and 'Dykes, do that.' Late in the season, he kept me in the clubhouse almost until game time, giving me instructions. Finally, I said, 'If you don't mind, Mr. Miles, it's 10 minutes until game time, and I have to get out on the field.' 'Okay, Dykes,' Miles said. 'Go ahead.' So as I turned to leave, Mr. Miles called out, 'Before you get out there, Dykes, take that grass off the back of your pants.' I answered, 'That's not grass, Mr. Miles. That's mistletoe.'"

Dykes didn't have to worry about dealing with Miles for long. He was let go; and general manager Arthur Ehlers was demoted after one year and replaced with Paul Richards, who had quit as manager of the Chicago White Sox to take the job as manager and general manager of the Orioles—the first man in baseball to hold both jobs since John McGraw ran the New York Giants from 1902 to 1932.

To say he hit the ground running would be an understatement. In his second month on the job, Richards engineered a blockbuster 17-player trade—still the largest in the history of baseball—that would shake up the baseball world and put Orioles fans on notice that they would not be doing business like the St. Louis Browns anymore.

The deal consisted of the Orioles trading pitcher Don Larsen, Bob Turley, and Mike Blyzka; first baseman Dick Kryhoski; shortstop Billy Hunter; catcher Darrell Johnson; and outfielder Jim Fridley to the New York Yankees for pitchers Jim McDonald, Bill Miller, and Harry Byrd; catchers Gus Triandos and Hal Smith; outfielder Gene Woodling; shortstop Willie Miranda; third baseman Kal Segrist; and second baseman Don Leppert and minor league outfielder Ted del Guercio.

Richards made an immediate impact, and he would continue to make an impact on the Orioles franchise for many years to come.

The Richards Influence

Paul Richards was a catcher in the major leagues. Not a particularly outstanding one, but decent enough to play eight major league seasons as a reserve catcher. But catchers are often students of the game, and Richards was no backup student. He was at the head of the class.

He began his managing career with the minor league Atlanta Crackers after retiring, and even went back to play for the Detroit Tigers in the 1945 World Series, when the playing ranks were depleted due to World War II. Richards went back to minor league managing shortly thereafter and got his break in the majors in 1951, when he was hired to manage the Chicago White Sox. He had some measure of success there with four winning seasons, but like every other American League team, he had the Yankees to deal with. New York won three straight pennants; then the Indians captured the flag in 1954.

Richards had seen enough of the Orioles—and the former St. Louis Browns—to be convinced that he had to shake things up when he arrived, which led him to the 17-player trade. He felt that any team that had lost 100 games in the previous two seasons needed drastic change.

The changes would not immediately make a strong impact. The 1955 Orioles won just three more games, going 57–97, and finished last in hitting and fielding in the American League. There was hope at the end of the season, though. They won 15 of their final 20 games, and there was a brief appearance by a youngster from Arkansas who years later would help put Baltimore baseball on the map.

Brooks Robinson was 18, only three months removed from his high school graduation, when he made his debut in Baltimore. The Orioles had signed him as a second baseman and gave him a $4,000 bonus. He spent the summer playing minor league ball in York, Pennsylvania, where manager George Staller converted him to third base.

"The Orioles brought me up at the end of the year," Brooks Robinson said. "I came to the park [on September 17, 1955] and the third baseman had gotten hurt. Paul Richards just told me I was playing."

He got two hits against the Washington Senators, went back to his room at the Southern Hotel, called his parents in Arkansas, and told them the major leagues were easy. But he would go back to the minors for seasoning and wouldn't return to Baltimore for good until four years later.

Richards continued to try to build the Orioles farm system, using controversial signing bonuses to lure young players like Ron Hansen, Chuck Estrada, Fred Valentine, and Chuck Hinton in 1956—all future major league players. He continued with such gems as pitchers Milt Pappas, Jack Fisher, and Steve Barber in 1957. His eye for talent landed Pete Ward, Jerry Adair, and a signing that would capture the headlines on sports pages across the country—a power-hitting prospect named Dave Nicholson, whom the Orioles signed for a $100,000 bonus.

There was one young pitcher the Orioles signed in 1957 for a lot less than $100,000. Scout Frank McGowan signed a hard-throwing right-hander named Steve Dalkowski out of high school for $10,000 and a new Pontiac. At first the Orioles thought they had signed the second coming of Walter Johnson, because Steve Dalkowski threw harder than anyone had ever seen in baseball.

"Ask anyone from that time who the fastest ever was," said Ray Youngdahl, a minor league teammate. "They'll tell you Dalkowski. He just had the gift. I've faced Sandy Koufax, and I'll tell you what: he wasn't faster than Steve."

"Best arm I've ever seen," said former Orioles pitcher and legendary general manager Pat Gillick, a minor league roommate of Dalkowski's. "He was a phenomenon. If he ever could have controlled himself, he would have been great."

Dalkowski once threw a pitch clear through the welded mesh backstop of a Wilson, North Carolina, grandstand. In Miami, Florida, he uncorked a wild throw that hit a fan at a concession stand. In Kingsport, Tennessee, Dalkowski tossed a 24-strikeout no-hitter, but walked 18 and lost the game, 8–4. He once tore off a batter's earlobe with a pitch. The batter ended up in the hospital and never played

Memorial Stadium, shown in September 1960, was the Orioles' nest from 1954 until 1991. It hosted one All-Star Game and 38 postseason games.

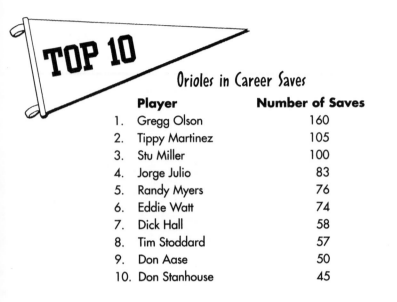

TOP 10

Orioles in Career Saves

	Player	Number of Saves
1.	Gregg Olson	160
2.	Tippy Martinez	105
3.	Stu Miller	100
4.	Jorge Julio	83
5.	Randy Myers	76
6.	Eddie Watt	74
7.	Dick Hall	58
8.	Tim Stoddard	57
9.	Don Aase	50
10.	Don Stanhouse	45

again. As a rookie in the Appalachian League, Dalkowski struck out 121 batters and walked 129 in 62 innings, going 1–8 with an 8.13 ERA.

Dalkowski never pitched for the Orioles, yet he remains very much an Orioles legend. Baltimore club officials put Dalkowski through a series of experiments to get him under control. One manager had him throw 75 to 100 pitches in the bullpen before each start to tire him out. Another gave him a thick-lensed pair of glasses to correct his 20-80/20-60 vision (which left him squinting at the plate). A third had him pitch to two batters on each side of the plate at the same time. Richards built a wooden target for Dalkowski, complete with a strike-zone-sized hole. By the time he had gone through a bag of balls, he had shattered the target.

Earl Weaver—his manager in Elmira, New York, in 1962—finally managed to get Dalkowski under control. In 160 innings pitched, Dalkowski recorded 192 strikeouts, 114 walks, and a 3.04 ERA, more than two runs per game lower than his previous best. In his final 57 innings, Weaver claimed that he struck out 110, walked 11, and had a 0.11 ERA. He appeared to be on the brink of finally pitching for the major league club.

In March 1963, Dalkowski tossed six innings of hitless spring training relief, and the Orioles told him he had made the club. But on

March 23, against the Yankees in the sixth inning, Dalkowski threw a slider to Phil Linz and felt a pop in his elbow. "I don't know how I knew it, but I knew my career was over right there," he said.

Richards was aggressive in his search for talent and his efforts to bring in new players, sometimes outrageously. In 1956, Richards made an offer to trade his entire 25-man roster with the Kansas City Athletics. The deal fell through when the Athletics refused to include two young prospects in the trade—outfielder Roger Maris and third baseman Clete Boyer.

Yes, if this transaction had somehow taken place, Brooks Robinson might have found himself trying to make a team with an already-outstanding third baseman—Boyer. Someone would have had to change positions, and it might have changed baseball history.

The progress was slow but steady. They moved up from seventh to sixth place in 1956, and improved their record to 69–85. The growth took a big jump in 1957, when the once hapless Orioles finished with a .500 record, going 76–76 and climbing to fifth in the American League. They took a small step back in 1958 and 1959, dropping to 74 wins both seasons. But they kept closing the gap between themselves and the pennant winners.

Gus Triandos had become a fan favorite, tying the league record for home runs by a catcher in a season, hitting 30 in 1958. He was one of two Orioles who would get to play before their hometown fans in the All-Star Game that year, which was played at Memorial Stadium in Baltimore. Orioles fans got a chance to see such great National League players as Stan Musial, Willie Mays, and Hank Aaron. The other Bird was pitcher Billy O'Dell, who wound up picking up the save in a 4–3 American League win before a crowd of nearly 49,000 fans. O'Dell, who pitched the final three innings of scoreless relief, was named the game's Most Valuable Player.

The 1958 season also saw the arrival of Brooks Robinson as the starting third baseman. He struggled at the plate, batting .238 in 145 games, but under the tutelage of George Kell

TRIVIA

Who was the first Oriole to play in an All-Star Game?

Answers to the trivia questions are on pages 165–166.

IF ONLY . . . Baltimore fans had known Hoyt Wilhelm was going to pitch the first no-hitter in Orioles history on September 20, 1958, there might have been more than 11,000 people at Memorial Stadium that day to watch it. Wilhelm, who became a Hall of Famer as a reliever, used his famous knuckleball as a starter that day to beat the New York Yankees, 1–0. Fans could take heart—at least it was a nationally televised game.

he began to develop into a standout third baseman, though no one knew then that he would go beyond standout and eventually become the greatest third baseman in the history of the game.

Another change would take place in the way the Orioles operated. Richards had been acting as both manager and general manager, but now would confine his duties to the dugout. The owners were not pleased with the liberal way he was spending money, and the $100,000 bonus for Dave Nicholson was the last straw. There were also tensions between Richards and the director of scouting, Jim McLaughlin, who often used a network of his own private scouts to sign players. McLaughlin was the only member of the Browns front office to move to Baltimore. His biggest impact may have been bringing a young minor league manager named Earl Weaver into the system in 1957.

The Orioles brought in Lee MacPhail to be their new general manager in 1958. The son of flamboyant former Brooklyn Dodgers owner Larry MacPhail, Lee was director of player personnel for the New York Yankees from 1948 through 1958, helping to develop teams that won nine pennants in those years. He came to Baltimore and continued to do the work that Richards had been doing. He signed Boog Powell and Dean Chance in 1959; Andy Etchebarren, Eddie Watt, Darold Knowles, and Larry Haney in 1960; Davey Johnson and Mark Belanger in 1962; and then Wally Bunker and Jim Palmer in 1963. This was the blueprint that Richards laid out and MacPhail followed, the blueprint that would make the Orioles a model franchise for years to come.

One change MacPhail would make was to move spring training. After three straight years in Scottsdale, Arizona, MacPhail moved spring training to Miami in 1959, where it would remain until 1990.

Building a Franchise

Paul Richards was always looking for an edge for his team, in the front office and on the field as well. Once, in a 1958 game against the Kansas City Athletics, Richards listed three pitchers in his starting lineup. He was hoping for a scoring chance in the first inning, at which point he could remove the extra pitchers for the batter of his choice: Billy O'Dell batting ninth as the pitcher, Jack Harshman in center field batting fifth, and Milt Pappas at second base batting seventh. It didn't work. Only O'Dell batted, in a 7–1 loss.

Two years later Richards developed an oversized catcher's mitt to handle Hoyt Wilhelm's knuckleball (the Orioles had 38 passed balls the year before when Wilhelm was pitching). The glove was one and a half times as large as the standard glove and 40 ounces heavier, and it was used in a May 27 game against the Yankees. Wilhelm pitched a complete-game 3–2 win at Yankee Stadium, with no passed balls by catcher Clint Courtney.

Wilhelm came to Baltimore on waivers from the Cleveland Indians in August 1958. He had been a reliever throughout his career, but the Indians began using him as a starter that season, and he maintained that position with the Orioles. One month after joining the Orioles, on September 20, 1958, pitching in the rain on national television, Wilhelm no-hit the Yankees 1–0, in a game that took just one hour and 48 minutes. Former Orioles starter Don Larsen allowed just one hit through six innings for New York in a 0–0 game. Gus Triandos homered off reliever Bobby Shantz for the win—Wilhelm's only victory for the Orioles that year. But at the age of 36, Wilhelm was a standout starter for the Orioles in 1959, going 15–11 with a 2.19 ERA, the best in the league—even with all the passed balls that year.

TRIVIA

Who won Rookie of the Year in the American League in 1960?

Answers to the trivia questions are on pages 165–166.

There was much to feel good about with these Baltimore Orioles after the 1959 season. Robinson began hitting better, batting .284 in 88 games. The "Baby Birds" pitching staff of Milt Pappas, Jack Fisher, Jerry Walker, and others showed a lot of promise. The trio of 20-year-old pitchers participated in two double-shutout victories during the season. Pappas and Walker shut out the Senators by the scores of 8–0 and 5–0 in July, and then two months later Fisher and Walker blanked the White Sox, 3–0 and 1–0; the latter being a remarkable 16-inning performance by Walker, who threw about 170 pitches. The promise turned into results in 1960 when the Orioles turned in their best record to date, finishing in second place, eight games behind the pennant-winning Yankees, with a record of 89–65, drawing their highest attendance yet of 1,187,849 fans at Memorial Stadium—an impressive number in a football town ruled by the Baltimore Colts.

They were in the race right to the final month, and on September 2, when Milt Pappas threw a three-hit shutout in a 5–0 win over the Yankees, the Orioles trailed New York by just .003 points. However, two weeks later they were swept in a four-game series by the Yankees, dropping them four games back and out of the pennant race.

There was much to feel good about when the 1960 season ended. Brooks Robinson continued to shine at third base and improve at the plate. At one point he was getting eight straight hits, including going 5 for 5 and hitting for the cycle in a July 15, 1960, game against the Chicago White Sox, a 5–2 win. Robinson would hit 14 home runs, drive in 88 runs, and bat .294. He was part of an offense that consisted of six players with double figures in home runs, led by shortstop Ron Hansen with 22 home runs and 86 RBIs and first baseman Jim Gentile with 21 home runs and 98 RBIs.

The Baby Birds pitching staff had sprouted their wings, as five starters got double-digit victories, led by Chuck Estrada (18–11) and Pappas, who posted a 15–11 mark. Pappas was a brilliant pitcher but had gained a reputation of being difficult, showing up umpires on calls, and once calling the press box during a game to complain about an official scorer's decision that had cost him four earned runs. But he was often worth the grousing. On June 19 of that 1960 season, Pappas and Hoyt Wilhelm threw a doubleheader shutout to beat the Tigers in Detroit. Wilhelm won the opener, 2–0, on a two-hitter, while Pappas gave up just three hits in winning the nightcap by the score of 1–0.

In the opening game of that doubleheader, catcher Clint Courtney, using the oversized glove to catch Wilhelm, was called twice for catcher's interference. It was a struggle for Courtney to catch Wilhelm because Courtney struggled with pretty much everything. He was a big, strong country boy from Louisiana whose eccentricities, such as lying in bed and spitting at the ceiling, drove his teammates crazy. He was the first big-league catcher to wear

Hoyt Wilhelm, one of the first Orioles to make the Hall of Fame (in 1985), was a three-time All-Star for Baltimore.

JAMES HOYT WILHELM
NEW YORK N.L., 1952-1956 ST. LOUIS N.L., 1957
CLEVELAND A.L., 1957-1958 BALTIMORE A.L., 1958-1962
CHICAGO A.L., 1963-1968 CALIFORNIA A.L., 1969
ATLANTA N.L., 1969-1970, 1971 CHICAGO N.L., 1970
LOS ANGELES N.L., 1971-1972
BASEBALL'S PREMIER RELIEF PITCHER. USED KNUCKLE BALL TO WIN 143 GAMES (A RECORD 124 IN RELIEF) AND AMASSED 227 SAVES OVER 21-YEAR CAREER. NO-HIT YANKEES ON SEPT. 20, 1958 IN INFREQUENT START FOR ORIOLES. PITCHED IN RECORD 1070 GAMES WITH LIFETIME ERA OF 2.52.

TRIVIA

Which two Orioles shortstops have identical career stolen-base marks with the club?

Answers to the trivia questions are on pages 165–166.

glasses on the field—thick Coke-bottle lenses. He once bet Whitey Herzog a fifth of booze that Wilhelm would not throw one past him behind the plate. "In the second inning, a pitch comes in, hits Clint on the top of his cap, and bounces in front of the plate," Herzog said. "He turned to the dugout and yelled, 'See, it didn't get by.'"

The improvement continued in 1961, when the Orioles put together what should have been a pennant-winning season, going 95–67, led by the slugging of first baseman Jim Gentile, who blasted 46 home runs—including two consecutive grand slams on May 9—and drove in 141 runs. This was the year of expansion in the American League, and the Orioles weren't the only ones who bene-fited from beating up on the weak new opposition. They finished third in the American League, 14 games behind the first-place Yankees, and the Paul Richards era of the Orioles ended in September, when he resigned with 27 games left in the season to become the general manager of the new Houston Colt 45s National League expansion team the next year. Lum Harris finished the season with a 17–10 record, and Billy Hitchcock would be the new Baltimore manager in 1962.

The Orioles would play a role in the historic season Yankees out-fielder Roger Maris was having, chasing Babe Ruth's single-season home-run mark of 60. On September 20, Baltimore played New York in the Yankees' 154th game of the season, which, according to Commissioner Ford Frick, was Maris's last chance to beat Ruth. Frick, Ruth's former biographer, declared that for the record to be broken, Maris must do it in the same number of games as Ruth. Maris hit his 59th home run of the year off Pappas, officially falling short of the record and resulting in the asterisk affixed by Frick on Maris's record of 61 home runs. Thirty-seven years later, Pappas said in an interview that he told Maris the night before the game that if the game's outcome was not on the line, he would throw him nothing but fastballs. Six days later, in game 159 of the 1961 season at Yankee Stadium, Orioles pitcher Jack Fisher gave up Maris's 60th home run, tying Ruth's mark.

Improvements were also taking place in towns far away from Baltimore, like Rochester, New York, and other Orioles farm clubs, with the promotion of Harry Dalton from assistant farm director to the head of minor league operations. The system would produce such future stars as Davey Johnson and Jim Palmer under Dalton's watch. In the first four years he was in charge of the farm system, the Orioles' minor league teams won nine pennants. In 1964, they had the best collective won-lost percentage in baseball (.565). He was the future of the Baltimore Orioles.

There wouldn't be quite as many games on the line in 1962, as the Orioles fell back to 77–85 with Hitchcock as the skipper, finishing in seventh place. The losing season took its toll at the ticket window, as the club dropped to 790,254, down nearly 300,000 from the high of 1960. One new arrival that would have an impact beyond wins and losses was Robin Roberts, at the end of his Hall of Fame career. He would have a major influence on a number of young Orioles pitchers, particularly Jim Palmer. "For whatever reason, Robin Roberts was willing to share with me, and I wanted to learn," Palmer said—a practice that Palmer would pass on when he became the aging veteran.

On August 26, Roberts, who had been released earlier in the year by the Yankees, defeated Whitey Ford 2–1 on home runs by Brooks Robinson and Jim Gentile to complete a five-game Orioles sweep of the Yankees.

Another new face was a young, big-slugging outfielder/first baseman who went by the nickname "Boog." John Wesley "Boog" Powell, at 6'4" and 240 pounds, would hit 15 home runs and drive in 53 runs in 124 games. The big redhead would become one of the favorites at Memorial Stadium, with his colorful sense of humor and mammoth home runs, of which there would be many.

They rebounded in 1963, posting an 86–76 mark, but Hitchcock was fired at the end of the season and replaced with his third-base coach, former Yankees outfielder Hank Bauer, for the 1964 season. Bauer would pay immediate dividends, as Baltimore proved it was

In 1961, Orioles first baseman Diamond Jim Gentile hit five grand-slam home runs, tying a major league record, including two in consecutive innings on May 9 in a 13–5 win over the Minnesota Twins.

heading back in the right direction. They posted a franchise-best won-loss record of 97–65, finishing in third place in a closely contested pennant race that saw them just two games behind the Yankees and a game behind the second-place Chicago White Sox. They had occupied first place for 87 days and were there as late as September 16. Bauer was named AL Manager of the Year for the team's run at the pennant.

This was the year that Brooks Robinson would gain national attention as one of the premier players in the American League, winning Most Valuable Player honors, batting .317 with 28 home runs and 118 RBIs, winning his fifth Gold Glove, and playing in his eighth straight All-Star Game. He became a fan favorite and took hold as the identity of baseball in Baltimore, alongside Johnny Unitas as the face of football in the city. Boog Powell led the team with 39 home runs, and the veterans Pappas (16–7) and Roberts (who, with a 13–7 record, showed he still had some gas left in the tank) were joined by a 19-year-old rookie named Wally Bunker, who compiled a 19–5 record. The bullpen may have been the best in the league, led by Stu Miller, who went 7–7 with 23 saves and a 3.06 ERA, and Dick Hall, who had a 9–1 mark with seven saves and a 1.85 ERA. Attendance shot back up to 1,116,215 fans coming through the turnstiles at Memorial Stadium.

The 1964 season was a watershed year in American League baseball. It marked the end of the Yankees era, as New York lost in seven games to the St. Louis Cardinals in the 1964 World Series, and would not return to the fall classic for 12 years. And it also marked the beginning of excellence for the Orioles franchise.

They nearly matched their record in 1965, going 94–68 but finishing third behind the pennant-winning Minnesota Twins. They had come close for two years running now, and the pieces were falling into place. Another piece of the puzzle arrived in 1965 when Jim Palmer joined the staff. His first win was worth noting, a 7–5 victory on May 16 against the Yankees, as Palmer himself supplied the winning margin with a two-run home run off Jim Bouton. He would finish the season with a 5–4 mark.

A series of front office changes, starting with the ownership, took place when the 1965 season ended. National Brewing Company President Jerold Hoffberger became chairman of the board and club president. Frank Cashen, a former sportswriter serving at the time as the brewery director of advertising, became the Orioles' executive vice president. Harry Dalton was named director of player personnel.

With the Yankees franchise collapsing, the door was open for a number of other American League teams. The Baltimore Orioles went to the front of the line with a trade they made on December 9, 1965, that would change the course of baseball in Baltimore.

Brooks Robinson

The record shows that the Baltimore Orioles franchise as it is currently constituted began when the St. Louis Browns moved to Baltimore for the 1954 season. But for all intents and purposes, the franchise really was born on May 28, 1955, in Little Rock, Arkansas, when a star high-school athlete named Brooks Calvert Robinson signed a contract to play for the Orioles.

Before he was done playing in 1977, Brooks Robinson would establish himself as the greatest third baseman of all time—known as the "human vacuum cleaner"—and, as one of the most beloved figures in the city of Baltimore, given another nickname: "Mr. Oriole."

The 18-year-old kid, in a meeting with Arthur Ehlers, the assistant to general manager/manager Paul Richards, signed for a bonus of $4,000. He didn't play high school baseball because his school didn't have a team—he played basketball and football—but he caught the eye of many major league scouts while playing American Legion baseball.

Thirteen teams were courting Robinson, but he chose the dismal Orioles. "I figured it represented my best chance to make the major leagues," he said.

Robinson got on a plane to Baltimore, where he joined the major league club for a few games before he was scheduled to be assigned to the minor league team in nearby York, Pennsylvania. He worked out with the team at second base before their game against the Yankees at Memorial Stadium, where Richards determined they would use him.

Soon Robinson began playing second base for the York White Roses. After two months, White Roses manager George Staller moved him to third base. Robinson made a strong impression, hitting 11 home runs and batting .331 in 95 games, and he got the call—at the age of 18—to the major league club on September 17. Robinson played in place of injured third baseman Kal Segrist against the Washington Senators, and went 2 for 4. But he went 0 for 18 for the rest of the season, and was sent back down to the minor leagues for the 1956 season.

"I told them I didn't know why I'd been in York all year," Robinson said. "Then I went 0 for 19 [actually 18] with 10 strikeouts the rest of the season."

After several brief call-ups in 1956 and 1957, Robinson came up and played in 145 games in 1958, but batted just .238 with only three home runs and 32 RBIs. He would split time between Baltimore and

Brooks Robinson, here making a diving catch of Johnny Bench's line drive in Game 5 of the 1970 World Series against the Reds, earned 15 Gold Gloves at third and won the 1964 American League MVP.

TOP 10

Players with Most Games Played for the Orioles

	Player	Games
1.	Cal Ripken Jr.	3,001
2.	Brooks Robinson	2,896
3.	Mark Belanger	1,962
4.	Eddie Murray	1,884
5.	Boog Powell	1,763
6.	Brady Anderson	1,759
7.	Paul Blair	1,700
8.	Ken Singleton	1,446
9.	Al Bumbry	1,428
10.	Rick Dempsey	1,245

Class AAA Vancouver in 1959, then come up for good in 1960, batting .294 with 14 home runs and 88 RBIs, good enough to be named Most Valuable Player on the team. He also won the first of 16 consecutive Gold Glove awards.

He was named to the first of 18 All-Star Games in 1961 and established himself as a third baseman with some power, hitting 23 home runs, driving in 86 runs, and batting .303 in 1962.

Two years later Robinson had his career year, slugging 28 home runs, driving in 118 runs, and batting .317. He won American League MVP honors, and the Orioles had their best season yet, winning 97 games and finishing two games out of first place behind the pennant-winning New York Yankees. The team won 94 games the following season, with Robinson hitting 18 home runs and driving in 80 runs. And they were building a powerful lineup, with a young slugger named Boog Powell and second baseman Davey Johnson. But in 1966 they added another Robinson—this one named Frank—in a trade with the Cincinnati Reds, and the two Robinsons, who became good friends, led the Orioles to their first World Series championship, stunning the defending champion Los Angeles Dodgers by sweeping them in four games. It was the beginning of an era of excellence in Orioles baseball, and Brooks Robinson symbolized that as much as anybody.

He continued to be named to All-Star teams and win Gold Gloves as the Orioles either won the AL pennant or competed for it throughout the rest of the decade. Then, at the 1970 World Series, when baseball was getting more exposure on national television, Robinson took center stage and captured the attention of the country with his stunning play at third base and his clutch hitting. He was named the Series MVP after batting .429 with two home runs and six RBIs. Baltimore won its second World Series championship by defeating the Cincinnati Reds in five games.

His play at third base prompted Reds manager Sparky Anderson to say during the Series, "I'm beginning to see Brooks in my sleep. If I dropped this paper plate, he'd pick it up on one hop and throw me out at first."

Robinson acknowledged he played perhaps the best baseball of his career during that Series. "I just happened to be in the right spot in that Series," he said. "I tell people that I played 23 seasons and I never did have five games in a row like I did in that World Series. As an infielder you can go a week or two and never get a chance to do something spectacular. In this Series, every game I had a chance to do something outstanding defensively and I was hitting well, too. It was a once-in-a-lifetime five-game Series for me and it just happened to be in a World Series."

The world was impressed, but for Orioles fans and Robinson's teammates, it was just validation of what they had seen with their own eyes for years. "What we saw in the World Series was spectacular, but we saw that on a daily basis," Boog Powell said. "It would take a .22-caliber rifle aimed in just the right way to get one past him. Brooks worked hard, even though the game came so easily to him. He'd drive in the big run. He was a champion at it. You wanted him up there in the late innings. I'd rather have him up there instead of me."

The Orioles and Robinson came close to repeating in 1971, but that World Series was a stage for Roberto Clemente, as the Pittsburgh Pirates outfielder led his team to victory in seven games. It would be Robinson's last appearance in the World Series.

TRIVIA

What major league record does Brooks Robinson hold that he would gladly give up?

Answers to the trivia questions are on pages 165–166.

Baltimore would continue to compete, winning the AL East division title in 1973 and 1974, but Robinson's offensive numbers were declining—he never hit double-digit home runs in a season after slugging 20 in 1971—and he called it quits on August 25, 1977, after playing in just 24 games in 1977 and batting .149. It was a new era in Baltimore baseball, with stars coming up like Eddie Murray.

A crowd of more than 51,000 turned out on September 18 to honor Robinson, as the Orioles held a "Thank Brooks Day." Five years later, he would be inducted into the National Baseball Hall of Fame. The Orioles made the trip to play in the annual exhibition game at Cooperstown, and were accompanied by thousands of Baltimore fans who made the trek to honor their legendary third baseman. "I must be the luckiest man in the world," Robinson told the crowd. "I keep asking, 'How could any one man be so fortunate?' It's more than any one human being could ask for...one of my blessings was to play in Baltimore. I share this day with my adopted hometown, which supported Brooks Robinson on good and bad days. Baltimore, thank you, I love you all."

He had left the game having hit 268 career home runs and driving in 1,357 runs. He won 16 straight Gold Glove honors, sharing the record with pitcher Jim Kaat. He played in 18 All-Star Games. Brooks Robinson is still the gold standard for the position of third baseman.

Frank Arrives

How could anyone who knew Frank Robinson believe he would be finished as a ballplayer by the age of 30?

That's the story that came out in the winter of 1965, when Cincinnati Reds owner Bill DeWitt Sr. declared that Robinson was an "old 30." In a trade engineered by outgoing general manager Lee MacPhail, who was moving on to become American League president, and new GM Harry Dalton, DeWitt traded Robinson to the Baltimore Orioles on December 9 for pitchers Milt Pappas and Jack Baldschun and outfielder Dick Simpson.

Frank Robinson may have been the toughest and hardest ballplayer in baseball for the first 10 years of his career—and among the best. To think that Frank Robinson would suddenly fall off a cliff at the age of 30 was patently ridiculous then and, looking back 40 years later, an error in judgment of historic proportions for the Reds and good fortune of historic proportions for the Orioles.

Frank Robinson didn't stop playing for another 11 years, and he wasn't even an old 41 when he finally retired from active duty.

Born in Beaumont, Texas, on August 31, 1935, Frank Robinson took the National League and Cincinnati by storm as a rookie in 1956, hitting 38 home runs, scoring 122 runs, driving in 83 runs, and batting .290 in 152 games as the Reds, left fielder. He reeled off All-Star seasons, including leading the Reds to the NL pennant in 1961, and hit 324 home runs, drove in 1,009 runs, and batted .303 over 10 years in Cincinnati.

On the short list of great major league ballplayers—including Hank Aaron, Willie Mays, and Mickey Mantle—is the name Frank Robinson. His final year in Cincinnati gave no indication that he was slipping—33 home runs, 113 RBIs, and a .296 average. So he was stunned when he got the phone call that he had been traded to Baltimore.

He was stunned and determined to prove the Reds wrong, not that Robinson needed any outside motivation for performing at a high level. "It probably made me more determined than normal, but I always wanted to have a good year," Frank Robinson said. "I guess DeWitt's comment may have given me a little extra urge, especially at the start of the season."

Frank Robinson made his presence felt from the first day he reported to camp, when he hit a double as a pinch-hitter during an intrasquad game. A young Jim Palmer was certainly impressed when he saw Frank Robinson get a rocket shot off in an intrasquad game against a young pitcher named Steve Cosgrove with a tremendous curveball. "I turned to Dick Hall and said, 'I think we just won the pennant,'" Palmer said.

He made his presence felt off the field from the start, filling the void of clubhouse leadership and demanding hustle and heart from those who played with him. He was the "judge" in the kangaroo courts for fines for players who committed some on- or off-field error in baseball judgment and etiquette—all in good fun, but meant to keep everyone focused on staying sharp.

There was some fear about how the two Robinsons—Frank and Brooks—might get along, since the dynamic of the clubhouse had now changed dramatically. After all, Brooks Robinson was the face of the Orioles, and some reporters speculated that there would be a clash between the two stars.

The clash never materialized. "The writers tried to drive a wedge between Brooks and I and make it like we were in competition for the leadership of the ballclub," Frank Robinson said. "But we had a strong bond from day one. We never had a cross word between us, never an angry word. I respected him and his space and what he had done for that organization and how long he had been there, and he respected my space. We grew to respect each other even more as the years went on, both as persons and players. We never had any problems."

Second baseman Davey Johnson, here singling against Dave Giusti in Game 2 of the 1971 World Series against the Pirates, was part of the best keystone combination in baseball at the end of the '60s and early '70s.

Brooks Robinson called Frank a great teammate. "He led by the way he played. We saw when he got to our club what a great player he was. We had a ball."

Hank Bauer was also having a ball putting a lineup out on the field every day that had Frank Robinson in the middle of it, surrounded by Brooks Robinson, first baseman Boog Powell, and outfielder Curt Blefary. In 26 exhibition games, the four combined for 24 home runs and 65 RBIs, and batted .340.

So it was a pleasure for Bauer to bring this lineup card to home plate on April 12 for Opening Day against the Boston Red Sox at Fenway Park: Luis Aparicio, shortstop; Curt Blefary, left field; Frank Robinson, right field; Brooks Robinson, third base: Boog Powell, first base; Davey Johnson, second base; Paul Blair, center field; Andy Etchebarren, catcher; and on the mound, Steve Barber. There are

540—The estimated distance in feet of the home run hit by Frank Robinson on May 8, 1966, against the Cleveland Indians. Robinson, facing Luis Tiant, hit a shot that wound up going out of Memorial Stadium—the first and only time in the ballpark's history. A flag was put up at the bleacher railing where the home run left the stadium. It simply said, "Here," and it flew there until the ballpark closed in 1991.

three National Baseball Hall of Fame members in that lineup, and seven Orioles Hall of Famers, in addition to Bauer, the manager.

The first time Frank Robinson came up to the plate, he was hit by a pitch from Earl Wilson—big surprise. Robinson's fearlessness at the plate was already legendary when he arrived in the American League. He had been hit in 18 games in Cincinnati the year before, and would be hit 10 more times that first year in the new league. When he was done playing. Frank Robinson had been hit by more pitches than anyone in recorded baseball history at the time—198 times.

On Opening Day, the Red Sox led 4–3 in the top of the ninth when Brooks Robinson hit a run-scoring single to tie the game at 4–4. The Orioles won 5–4 when Boston pitcher Jim Lonborg balked in the winning run with the bases loaded and two outs in the thirteenth inning. Stu Miller, who pitched four innings of relief, got the victory. They won the following game 8–1, then came home to Baltimore for the April 15 opener at Memorial Stadium against the New York Yankees.

There was much excitement and anticipation over their return, primarily based on the presence of Frank Robinson, who told reporters that he knew all eyes would be on him. "I know they'll be watching me real close and that they expect a lot out of me," Frank Robinson said.

Jerry Vale sang the National Anthem before a crowd of 35,624, who went home disappointed, as the Yankees defeated Baltimore 3–2 behind the complete-game victory by Fritz Peterson. Wally Bunker took the loss, surrendering a solo home run to Joe Pepitone as the difference-maker. They saw Frank Robinson hit a solo home run, his third in three games, coming in the bottom of the ninth off Peterson.

It was a historic day in Baltimore, though, because Orioles fans saw the first black umpire in major league history work the game. Emmett Ashford had been working in the minor leagues since 1951 when he finally was promoted to the major leagues in 1966. Four days earlier, he made his major league debut before a crowd of 44,468 at DC Stadium for the Cleveland Indians' 5–2 win over the Washington Senators.

The Orioles bounced back to beat the Yankees 7–2 the next day and went off on a record 10-game winning streak, finishing the month of April with an 11–1 mark. They would be 12–1 when they lost again, a 3–0 shutout to the Senators in Washington. Palmer took the loss, surrendering a home run to Frank Howard in the defeat. Though the Senators would be the perennial cellar dwellers in the league, the Orioles struggled against their geographic rivals throughout the 1965 and 1966 seasons, going just 19–17 against Washington. They were 14–4 on May 8 at home, facing the Cleveland Indians, who were also off to a fast start and tied with the Orioles for first place, when Frank Robinson hammered the first piece of his Orioles legacy in the first inning of the second game of a doubleheader facing a young Luis Tiant, who Frank Robinson was seeing for the first time and who had thrown three consecutive shutouts.

"The first pitch he threw me was a fastball down and in, and I swung and knew I hit it good," Robinson said. "I rounded the bases like I usually did, no fooling around, and went back to the dugout. The players said, 'That ball went completely out of the ballpark.' I said, 'Bull—get out of here.' I didn't really believe it until I went back to the outfield at the end of the inning and the crowd gave me a standing ovation."

The ball had gone out of Memorial Stadium and landed in the parking lot beyond the left-field stands—the only ball ever hit out of the ballpark, an estimated 540 feet.

That would be the highlight of the month of May for the Orioles, the worst month the team would have in the 1966 season. They finished that month with a 14–16 record, and had a record of 24–17 when they lost the final game of the month to the defending league champions, the Minnesota Twins, at Metropolitan Stadium. The losses and expectations did not weigh on the team, though, as they

TRIVIA

How many rookies started for the 1966 Orioles?

Answers to the trivia questions are on pages 165–166.

had one of the all-time characters on the squad to keep the team loose—reliever Moe Drabowsky.

Drabowsky came to the Orioles in 1966, where he would turn his career around and establish himself as one of the game's better relief pitchers. But he was better known for his sense of humor and bullpen pranks. The bullpen phone was his specialty. He would use it to order Chinese food to be delivered during games, and one night in Kansas City, he used it to mess with the Athletics bullpen.

Drabowsky had pitched in Kansas City before and knew the A's bullpen phone number. He called it in the second inning of a May 27 game, pretending to be Kansas City manager Al Dark, and told bullpen coach Bobby Hofman to get Lew Krausse ready. So Hofman got Krausse up to warm up. Not long after, Drabowsky called again and told Hofman, "Sit him down." Drabowsky then called the A's bullpen again, asked to speak to Krausse, and said, "You warm, Lew?" Krausse recognized the voice on the other end.

The incident made the papers the next day, but that didn't stop Drabowsky. Two days later, Drabowsky called the bullpen to speak to Hofman, pretending he was A's owner Charlie Finley. "This is Finley," he said. "I just got back in town and I saw that story in the paper Friday about the calls you got Friday night. I'd like to hear your version of the episode." Hofman began recounting the story, then got wise as the conversation went on and recognized Drabowsky.

Baltimore began June on a positive note, defeating the Twins in a 14–5 rout, with Etchebarren and Aparicio homering. They went 16–5 when they rolled into New York to face the Yankees on June 21, and were involved in a near riot in a 7–5 win over the Bronx Bombers in the first game of a doubleheader. Frank Robinson chased down a Roy White line drive in the bottom of the ninth inning—with two runners on base—that would have been a home run, except Frank Robinson fell into the seats as he caught the ball and disappeared. First base umpire Hank Soar had initially given the home run call but quickly changed it to an out when he determined Frank Robinson had indeed caught the ball. Yankees manager Ralph Houk stormed out of the dugout and threw a fit, kicking up dirt and throwing his cap. The fans at the ballpark were fired up, and took their anger out on Frank Robinson during the second game, throwing food, beer cans, firecrackers, and a host of other objects on the field during the game. "This is the worst crowd I have ever seen," Bauer, the former Yankees outfielder, told reporters. "Looks like we better play with machine guns." What was worse was that Frank Robinson went up against the right-field wall in the sixth inning to pull down a fly ball by Elston Howard. When a fan tried to interfere with him, Frank Robinson gave him an elbow in the ribs. They lost the second game 8–3, but took two of the next three from New York, three of four from the California Angels, and two out of three in Kansas City. They finished June with a 25–8 record and 50–25 overall.

Baltimore carried a 58–29 record and an eight-game first-place lead into the All-Star break. Brooks Robinson was the top vote-getter among American Leaguers in the All-Star balloting (the voting was done by players then), while Frank Robinson got the most votes among outfielders. Barber, with a 10–3 record, was named to the starting rotation, and catcher Etchebarren was named to the squad as well. They were the best of the best, and the Orioles representation at the All-Star Game showed they were the best. The National League would prevail 2–1 in 10 innings, but Brooks Robinson was named the game's Most Valuable Player. He had three hits, a triple and two singles, and set a record by handling eight chances at third base, including several highlight plays. He was the first member of a losing team to win the All-Star Game MVP.

Bringing a Championship Home

Going into the second half of the season, the best team in the league had problems. Steve Barber was on the disabled list with a sore elbow and would miss most of the rest of the year. Wally Bunker was sidelined with a sore elbow as well, and would pitch in just three games between the All-Star break and August 16. The list of pitching woes was a long one—Jim Palmer, Stu Miller, Eddie Watt, and Dick Hall all had various sorts of arm problems as well. The rest of the lineup in the second half didn't get off easy, either. Etchebarren broke a bone in his right hand on July 18 and missed 29 of the next 37 games. Powell suffered a fracture of his left ring finger when he was hit by a pitch on August 20, and hit just one home run in the last six weeks of the season. Johnson and Blefary also had stints on the disabled list. The injuries slowly took their toll. The Orioles went 19–10 in July, but just .500 (28–28) the rest of the year. They had built up enough of a cushion, though, to maintain their hold on first place and finish the season with a 97–63 record.

All of the hurts would have amounted to nothing if things had gone differently at a team pool party on August 22 (during an off day coming back from a three-game series in Detroit) at the home of, in an ironic twist, a Baltimore funeral home director. That was the night that the Orioles not only nearly lost the pennant, but almost lost Frank Robinson for good. Frank Robinson couldn't swim, but he changed into a swimsuit when his teammates threatened to throw him in with his clothes on. He tried to stay in the shallow end of the pool. "I was jumping up and down, hoping that would satisfy them and keep them away," Frank Robinson said. "But when I tried to regain my feet, I slipped into the deep end. I went down a couple of times and kept yelling for help when I surfaced. My wife was standing by the side of the pool, and she knows I can't swim. She thought I was kidding, and I guess everybody else did too."

Frank Robinson had gone down for the third time when finally someone—Andy Etchebarren—took it seriously. He jumped into the pool to save him. "I didn't take a deep breath when I first jumped in because I wasn't really sure if Frank was kidding," Etchebarren said. "When I realized he wasn't, I pushed him for a few yards and then resurfaced for air." Etchebarren finally got Frank Robinson to the side of the pool, where he lay for about five minutes before he recovered.

Moe Drabowsky, a bit of a flake but a darn good pitcher, delivers a pitch in Game 1 of the 1966 World Series against the Dodgers. The game was won in a sweep by the underdog Orioles.

TOP 10

Most Home Runs in a Season

	Player	Home Runs	Year
1.	Brady Anderson	50	1996
2.	Frank Robinson	49	1966
3.	Jim Gentile	46	1961
4.	Rafael Palmeiro	43	1998
5.	Boog Powell	39†	1964
	Rafael Palmeiro	39†	1995
	Rafael Palmeiro	39†	1996
8.	Rafael Palmeiro	38	1997
9.	Albert Belle	37†	1999
	Boog Powell	37†	1969

"The funny thing is what went through my mind," Frank Robinson said. "When Andy lost contact with me, I could see the headlines, 'Robinson Drowns at Team Party.'"

As if that weren't enough of a mess, the Frank Robinson incident happened while Powell was at the hospital being treated for a cut above his right eye—he had slipped while trying to toss Drabowsky into the pool.

The swimming pool incident seemed to unnerve the team. They had gone 6–2 in the previous eight games. They lost to the Indians in the game following the pool party, 2–1, and went 3–8 in the next 11 games, dropping to 83–51. But they started a six-game winning streak with a 4–1 win over the White Sox in Chicago, thanks to a strong pitching performance by Bunker and a home run by Blefary, raising their season record to 89–51. They would need those winning streaks in the final weeks of the season as they managed to stay afloat until clinching the pennant with a 6–1 win over the Athletics in Kansas City. Palmer got the win. Frank Robinson had three hits and drove in two runs, and Brooks Robinson also drove in two runs. They celebrated in the Orioles clubhouse, tossing owner Jerry Hoffberger into the showers. But before they did that, Hoffberger made several phone calls. One of them was to Reds owner Bill

DeWitt. "Years ago, when I saw you at a baseball meeting, I knew you were going to help me, and you did," Hoffberger said, recounting the conversation to reporters. "I really want to thank you, and I appreciate everything you've done for us."

This is what Bill DeWitt did for Jerry Hoffberger: He gave him the American League Triple Crown winner. He gave him the American League Most Valuable Player. He gave him the player who would take the Orioles franchise into an era of excellence.

Frank Robinson played in 155 games, scored 122 runs, and had 182 hits. He nailed 34 doubles, slammed 49 home runs, and drove in 122 runs. He batted .316. He was the leader of a powerful Orioles offense, supplemented by Powell and his 34 home runs and 109 RBIs, Brooks Robinson and his 23 home runs and 100 RBIs, and Blefary's 23 home runs. Palmer, with a 15–10 record, led a rotation that was hit hard by injuries that included a 13–6 record by McNally, 10–6 by Bunker, and 10–5 by Barber. No one was sure who would be healthy enough to pitch in the World Series.

The bullpen was Baltimore's salvation. Drabowsky may have been a prankster, but it didn't take away from his performance, as he went 6–0 with a 2.81 ERA and had seven saves in 44 games. The foursome of Miller, Hall, Eddie Fisher, and Gene Brabender combined for a 24–12 record and 40 saves. Hank Bauer, who presided over this championship squad, was named AL Manager of the Year. And the team had its best year yet at the box office, drawing 1,203,366 fans.

All of this added up to a 97–63 record, finishing ahead of the second-place Minnesota Twins by nine games. They would face a team in the World Series that was their opposite—the Los Angeles Dodgers, a team with legendary starting pitching and a weak offense. They were the defending world champions and had won two World Series championships in three seasons. They were led by one of the greatest left-handers of all time, Sandy Koufax, who posted a 27–9 mark and struck out 317 batters in 323 innings, pitching his way to another Cy Young Award. He wasn't the only future Hall of Fame hurler on that Dodgers team, though. Don Drysdale joined Koufax to give Los Angeles the best one-two pitching punch since the days of Warren Spahn and Johnny Sain, and the two Dodgers pitchers actually held out together in spring training in a dramatic dual holdout.

They held out for nearly all spring training before finally signing contracts—Koufax for $125,000 and Drysdale for $100,000. Drysdale would have an off year, with a 13–16 record. But Claude Osteen won 17 games, and a young hurler named Don Sutton won 12. The record that stood out was reliever Phil Regan's—otherwise known as "the Vulture" for the way he would swoop in and get victories. Regan went 14–1 in 1966. Managed by Walter Alston, who had led the Dodgers to four World Series championships, the Dodgers went 95–67, finishing one and a half games ahead of their rival, the San Francisco Giants, to win the National League, with an offense that hit just 108 home runs and scored 606 runs, compared to the 175 homers by Baltimore and 755 runs scored. Jim Lefebvre was their power hitter, with 24 home runs and 74 RBIs. They were a team built on pitching and the speed of base runners like Maury Wills, who had set the major league record for stolen bases in a season with 104 in 1962. He stole 38 bases in 1966, along with 21 steals by Willie Davis.

The Series opened at Dodger Stadium in Los Angeles on Wednesday, October 5, with Drysdale facing McNally. Frank Robinson did what he did from the first day he put on an Orioles uniform. He set the tone for the team with a two-run home run in the first inning. Brooks Robinson followed with a solo home run, and the Orioles led 3–0. The pitching for Baltimore would also mirror the way they won during the regular season. McNally struggled, giving up a solo home run to Lefebvre in the second inning and walked five batters through two and a third innings before he was taken out by Bauer and replaced by Drabowsky, who pitched a nearly perfect 6⅔ innings of relief, giving up just one hit, as Baltimore went on to win easily 5–2 before a crowd of 55,941.

Game 2 the next day was even easier against the great Koufax, who was betrayed in the fifth inning by his defense, as Willie Davis committed three errors in center field, allowing three unearned runs to score. Baltimore added a run in the sixth inning when Frank Robinson tripled and later scored on a single by Powell. Davey Johnson drove in two more in the eighth inning, while Jim Palmer allowed just four hits on his way to a 6–0 shutout victory. Koufax had been hurt by the errors, but he was not the same dominant pitcher, leaving after six innings with just two strikeouts, and the 55,947 fans

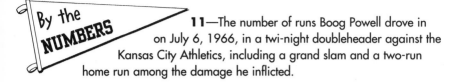

By the NUMBERS 11—The number of runs Boog Powell drove in on July 6, 1966, in a twi-night doubleheader against the Kansas City Athletics, including a grand slam and a two-run home run among the damage he inflicted.

at Dodger Stadium had no idea this would be the last time they would see Sandy Koufax pitch. He had suffered for years with arthritis in his pitching arm and called it a career after the 1966 season—165–87 wins, a 2.76 ERA, 2,396 strikeouts, and four no-hitters including a perfect game.

The Series came to Baltimore for Game 3 on Saturday, October 8, at Memorial Stadium before 54,445 fans, and this one came much harder for the Orioles than the first two. But they won Game 3 1–0 behind a six-hit complete-game outing by Bunker, the deciding run coming on a two-out, fifth inning solo home run by Paul Blair—one of just three hits by Baltimore in a game that lasted just 1 hour and 55 minutes. Now Baltimore—the hapless St. Louis Browns just 13 years before—were up 3–0 in the Series and on the verge of sweeping the defending champion Dodgers.

They would make the deciding game a memorable one—another masterful 1–0 pitching duel, this one by McNally, showing none of the control problems he had in Game 1, besting Drysdale. McNally gave up four hits while pitching a complete-game shutout. Drysdale gave up four hits over eight innings.

When Lou Johnson hit a fly ball to Blair for the third out in the top of the ninth inning, the Baltimore Orioles became world champions, and 54,458 fans in the world's largest outdoor insane asylum—the name given to Memorial Stadium when occupied by Baltimore Colt fans—went crazy.

The Orioles pitching staff were the stars. "I honestly didn't think we would get this kind of pitching," Bauer told reporters in the middle of the clubhouse celebration. "If there was a turning point, it was Drabowsky pitching like he did in the first game. He showed the rest of them what to do, and they just went and done it."

But ultimately, how was that fourth and final game decided? Who delivered the hit that cinched the World Series championship?

Who else? Frank Robinson, with a solo home run.

Optimism and Reality

There was nothing but blue skies on the horizon for the Baltimore Orioles baseball franchise after their 1966 World Series championship—or so it seemed. They had the best player in baseball coming off a career year, anchoring a powerful offense filled with young players and others in their prime, and a pitching staff with the same mixture.

There was good reason for optimism. The Orioles' two top farm clubs—Rochester in the International League and Elmira in the Eastern League—had won pennants in those leagues. The total record for the franchise's six farm teams was 388–316. Of the 55 players named to minor league All-Star teams in their respective leagues, 19 of them were Orioles prospects.

They would need those prospects. Player development was about to enter a new era, where teams would draft young talent instead of participating in the signing frenzies that dominated the days of Paul Richards.

"We have a chance for a dynasty if we can put together consecutive championships or be in the race strongly every year and win more than our share of championships—the way the Yankees, Dodgers, and Cardinals have in the past 25 years," general manager Harry Dalton told reporters, looking ahead. "But it will be more difficult to accomplish now, because under the current baseball legislation it will be harder to maintain a source of supply. From Baltimore's standpoint, both from its scouting staff and spending policy, we would be better off with no free agent draft. But within the framework of baseball, we believe this is helpful legislation and that is why we voted for it. If it helps baseball, we believe it will help us."

Dalton was a prophet. The Orioles were at the start of a time in the franchise when they would indeed be held up as a model like the Cardinals, Dodgers, and the Yankees. But he was also right that it would be more difficult to consistently replicate their success year in and year out.

The 1967 season would be a year out for the Baltimore Orioles. As right as everything seemed to go in 1966, that was as wrong as everything went in 1967. Barber never got over his arm problems and was traded to the Yankees before the All-Star break. Wally Bunker's physical woes also continued to plague him, and he was eventually banished to the bullpen. Palmer missed most of the year with shoulder problems. Stu Miller lost eight of his first nine decisions and posted a 3–10 mark. The one saving grace was rookie Tom Phoebus, who had led the International League in strikeouts in 1966 with 208. He won 14 games in 1967, but would never fulfill his potential in the major leagues.

Baltimore got off to a quick start in 1967, winning the first two games at Memorial Stadium against the Minnesota Twins and the first game of a three-game series at Kansas City against the Athletics. But after getting off to a 3–0 start, Baltimore went 6–14 in their next 20 games. After falling to 11–15, they seemed to

TRIVIA

Which Oriole was known in Japan as the "greatest leadoff man in the world"?

Answers to the trivia questions are on pages 165–166.

right the ship by going 6–1 in their next five games. In that stretch, the Orioles made history in a 12–8 win on May 17 over the Boston Red Sox.

They became the eighth club in American League history with four or more home runs in one inning when Andy Etchebarren, Sam Bowens, Boog Powell, and Davey Johnson connected in a nine-run seventh inning. Also homering for Baltimore was Frank Robinson, Brooks Robinson, and Paul Blair, the first time seven teammates have each homered. Boston's Carl Yastrzemski hit two homers, one coming in the bottom of the seventh; the total of five in one inning equals the ML record. Rounding out the round-trippers was Don Demeter for Boston.

Though the Orioles would come out on top of the Red Sox in

matchups when the season was over, winning 10 of their 18 games, it was the Red Sox who triumphed in the standings, beating out the Detroit Tigers and Minnesota Twins by one game to win the American League pennant for the first time since 1946. They were led by Yastrzemski, who turned in the league's second straight Triple Crown season, batting .326 with 44 home runs and 121 RBIs, and Jim Lonborg, who went 22–9. The "impossible dream" ended with a loss to Bob Gibson and the St. Louis Cardinals in seven games.

TRIVIA

How many different Orioles homered in a game against the Red Sox on May 17, 1967?

Answers to the trivia questions are on pages 165–166.

After beating up on the Senators and the Yankees, the Orioles suffered a frustrating loss to the Yankees at Yankee Stadium that would be an emotional setback. They were shut out, 2–0. A third-inning fly ball by Mickey Mantle had been caught by Frank Robinson in right field, but the ball popped out of his glove and over the fence for a home run.

Then on June 27, in a 5–0 loss to the White Sox, Frank Robinson was hurt in a second base collision with Al Weis. Frank Robinson suffered from double vision as a result and would wind up missing 28 games. Weis, a light-hitting utility infielder, would cause major headaches for the Orioles two years later. The Orioles were already sliding into a losing season when Frank Robinson went down because of their pitching problems. They were 32–36 when Frank Robinson was hurt; they were 43–53 when he returned.

Frank Robinson still finished the season with impressive numbers—30 home runs, 94 RBIs, and a .311 batting average. But his surrounding cast would not come close to matching Frank Robinson's offensive output, even in his injury-filled season. Brooks Robinson hit 22 home runs but drove in just 77 runs. And Boog Powell, who had blasted 39 home runs the year before, hit just 13 and drove in 55 runs in 125 games, also battling injuries.

The Orioles finished with an embarrassing 76–85 record, tied for sixth place with Washington (whose record was seen as progress under manager Gil Hodges), 15½ games out of first place. Their worst record against opposing teams was a preview of what the league would be facing in 1968. Baltimore lost 15 of 18 games to the Detroit Tigers, who would go on in 1968 to decisively win the pennant.

Baltimore had the kind of season in 1967 that usually results in changes being made, and in this case, Baltimore came close to firing their manager, but instead sent a message through the coaching staff. Pitching coach Harry Brecheen was fired and replaced with George Bamberger. Coaches Sherm Lollar and Gene Woodling were let go as well, and replaced with Ray Scarborough and the Class AAA Rochester manager from 1967—Earl Weaver.

There were player changes as well. Dalton traded shortstop veteran and fan favorite Luis Aparicio back to the White Sox, along with outfielders Russ Snyder and John Matias, in exchange for pitchers Bruce Howard, Roger Nelson, and outfielder Don Buford, who

Shortstop Luis Aparicio (left), with the White Sox's Nellie Fox in 1963, was traded back to the Sox in 1967, after leading the American League in stolen bases twice for the Orioles.

By the NUMBERS

1.95—The lowest ERA in a season by an Orioles pitcher, by Dave McNally in 1968.

would prove to be a valuable leadoff hitter for Baltimore for years to come. The deal also gave the slick-fielding Mark Belanger the Orioles shortstop position.

Baltimore opened the 1968 season with a 3–1 win over the relocated Athletics (moved to Oakland by controversial owner Charles Finley from Kansas City during the off season) at home, and won their second game of the year, 3–0, against the California Angels. After losing the next two, the Orioles traveled to Oakland for the Athletics' debut on April 17 at Oakland-Alameda County Coliseum. Dave McNally—who struggled with arm problems in 1967 and missed about 11 starts, posting a 7–7 record—gave every indication he was fully recovered by tossing a two-hitter in a 4–1 win over Oakland, in a stadium that left something to be desired by Major League Baseball standards. During the game, the dirt covering the pitching mound was kicked aside, exposing the steel frame of a shallow dome underneath, so the mound had to be recovered between innings.

Ten days later, Tom Phoebus, the Orioles' top pitcher in 1967, put his name in the record books with a 6–0 no-hitter against the defending American League champion, the Boston Red Sox. Brooks Robinson drove in three runs and saved the no-hitter in the eighth inning when he made a great catch to rob Rico Petrocelli of a hit in the eighth. What was noteworthy in the game was that converted outfielder Curt Blefary caught Phoebus behind the plate. Blefary wound up catching 40 games that year. He would only catch a total of 66 during his eight-year career.

Though the 1968 season was not unfolding as a repeat of 1967, the Orioles were still perceived as falling short of where they should be at the All-Star break, six games over .500 with a 43–37 record, and watching the Tigers, 10½ games ahead of them, run away with the pennant. The frustration resulted in the change that Dalton had delayed at the start of the season—firing manager Hank Bauer. Dalton replaced him with the 37-year-old Weaver, the fiery former minor league manager whom Dalton had been grooming to be the Orioles skipper.

Weaver, who bounced around the St. Louis Cardinals minor league system as a second baseman, started managing at the age of 26 as player-manager for the Knoxville Smokies of the South Atlantic League in 1956. He didn't do very well, going 10–24 during his stint in Knoxville, but Orioles director of scouting Jim McLaughlin saw enough to bring him into the Orioles farm system in 1957, where he managed the Class D team in Fitzgerald, Georgia, going 65–74 that season. It would be Weaver's last losing season until nearly 30 years later.

Weaver worked his way up the Orioles system and managed at Class AAA Rochester in 1966 and 1967 before being brought onto Bauer's staff in 1968. His teams had finished first or second in eight of the previous nine years he had managed. He had a reputation as a winner. But he also had a well-founded reputation as a walking explosion, a manager who battled umpires at every turn.

He also brought with him a modern sensibility for the game, as he was believed to be one of the first managers to rely heavily on statistics and matchups in his personnel decisions. At the end of the 1968 season, he asked Orioles public relations director Bob Brown how difficult it would be to break out statistics for how his players fared against specific pitchers, and how his pitchers fared against specific hitters. He would use those numbers to guide his decisions.

This was not the style of his predecessor Bauer. When second baseman Davey Johnson—a mathematics whiz who himself would go on to become a successful major league manager—presented Bauer with a computer printout he came up with in 1968 about how best he should be used based on the numbers against pitchers, he didn't find a receptive audience. "Hank told him to take the computer and stick it," Hendricks said.

The numbers added up pretty good once Weaver took over. The Orioles won 11 of their next 15 games and closed the gap between them and the league-leading Tigers. McNally led the charge. He defeated one of the Tigers' aces, Mickey Lolich, 5–1 in a July 28 game against Detroit. Nearly a month later, McNally hit a first-inning grand slam off Oakland's Chuck Dobson in an 8–2 victory over the

A's. On August 31, he won his 10th-straight game, beating the Tigers again 5–1.

They would not catch Detroit, though. This was the Tigers' year. You could see it coming by their 1967 finish, just one game out from first place. The Tigers left no doubt about the 1968 season, winning 103 games. They were led by Denny McLain, who became the major league's first 30-game winner since Dizzy Dean in 1934, going 31–6. With Lolich's 17–9 year, the Tigers, with former Baltimore native Al Kaline leading the offense, had the one-two punch on the mound to beat the defending champion St. Louis Cardinals, led by Bob Gibson's 22–9 record and his remarkable 1.12 ERA, in seven games in the World Series. It was McLain's 31 wins and Gibson's 1.12 ERA that helped change the game. The 1968 season was the last year of the pitcher. In light of the weak offensive numbers—Yastrzemski was the American League's only .300 hitter, winning the batting title with a .301 average, and there were only three players in either league with more than 100 RBIs—corresponding to the dominance of the pitchers, baseball decided to lower the mound after the season, diminishing the power of the pitcher and trying to generate more offense.

The Orioles rebounded from their dismal 1967 season and finished in second place with a 91–71 record—48–34 under Weaver. As with Detroit in 1967, the Orioles' resurgence in 1968 would be a sign of things to come in the 1969 season.

No Miracles

Baltimore made a major trade on December 4, 1968, that would make their strong starting rotation even more formidable. They traded outfielders Curt Blefary and John Mason to the Houston Astros for infielders Elijah Johnson and Enzo Hernandez and a left-handed pitcher with a nasty screwball and change-up who had gone 8–11 with the Astros in 1968—Mike Cuellar.

Cuellar had been a legendary pitcher in Cuba at the age of 18 when, in 1955, he pitched a no-hitter for Cuban dictator Fulgencio Batista's army team. Two years later, he was signed by the Havana Sugar Kings in the International League, where he struck out seven straight batters in his first start. But in six major league seasons, Cuellar turned in mediocre numbers—until he came to Baltimore and joined McNally and Palmer for an All-Star pitching staff.

The 1969 season would be a season of change. The Tigers were the last winners of the AL pennant as constituted under the old system. With the addition of expansion teams in Seattle (Pilots), San Diego (Padres), Montreal (Expos), and Kansas City (Royals), both leagues were broken up into divisions, the East and the West, and for the first time there would be a League Championship Series before the World Series.

There was an experiment in spring training that year, using what was called the "designated pinch-hitter." Powell was the DPH for the Orioles the first time it was used on March 6, batting ninth for the pitcher and driving in the winning run with a single in a 2–1 win over Minnesota. The experiment would last about three weeks. Four years later, the DPH became the DH, and became a permanent addition in the American League.

Baltimore opened the season with a 5–4 loss to the Boston Red Sox at Memorial Stadium. They came back and beat Boston 2–1 two days later. Then Washington came to town and beat the Orioles 4–0. The Orioles came back and won the second game 9–0. Game 5 of the 1969 season would be an important one for the Orioles—it would mark the return of Jim Palmer to a major league mound after suffering through two years of arm problems. The last time Palmer started for the Orioles was on September 19, 1967. He came back in style, pitching a five-hit 2–0 shutout against the Senators in the first game of a doubleheader. Baltimore shut out Washington 9–0 in the second game, but had an overall 11–0 shutout for the day. Traveling to Boston, the Orioles lost to the Red Sox, but came back to win 10–5 over the Red Sox the next day. Then on April 16 the Orioles won the series finale by a score of 11–8. Billy Conigliaro, playing in place of his brother Tony, hit two home runs for his first major league hits, but Blair, Buford, and Brooks Robinson also homered to lead the Orioles into first place in the American League East—where they would remain for the rest of the season.

Baltimore just rolled through the league after that. Five days later, Palmer won his third straight game, allowing just four hits, as the Orioles beat the Indians 11–0. Five days after that, the Orioles swept the Yankees in a doubleheader, 6–0 in a shutout by Cuellar, and 10–5. Frank Robinson had eight RBIs on the day. On May 15, McNally took a no-hit bid into the ninth inning when, with one out, Cesar Tovar singled, leaving the Orioles hurler with a one-hit 5–0 shutout.

McNally was nearly unhittable for much of 1969. He certainly appeared unbeatable. He went 10–0, pitching a two-hitter against the Senators in Washington on June 19 before President Richard Nixon. On July 5, a week before the All-Star break, McNally, who had won his last two decisions in 1968, won his 14th straight, giving him a 12–0 record for the 1969 season, in a 9–3 win over the Tigers in Detroit, stopping a three-game Orioles losing streak.

It wasn't until August 3 against the Twins that McNally finally lost, on a pinch-hit grand-slam home run by Rich Reese in a 5–2 defeat. It stopped McNally's winning streak at 17 games and gave him a record of 15–1 for the year. Remarkably, it would turn out that

McNally wasn't even considered the best pitcher that year for Baltimore. The pitcher they stole from Houston would be—not just for Baltimore, but in the entire American League. Cuellar had literally become unhittable in the final two months of the season. Tovar again had the only hit against an Orioles pitcher in a 2–0 win over the Twins on August 10.

The starting rotation for Baltimore was unlike any baseball had seen in quite some time. It sometimes appeared that one would somehow try to outdo the other. Three days after Cuellar's one-hitter, Palmer raised his record to 11–2 when he pitched an 8–0 no-hitter against the Oakland A's.

At this point, the Orioles juggernaut had a 14½ game lead in the AL East—and that lead would only grow. When the regular season ended, the Orioles had won the division by 19 games, with a franchise best 109–53. Cuellar would be the American League Cy Young co-winner (with Denny McLain), with a 23–11 record and a 2.38 ERA. McNally finished with a 20–7 record, while Palmer's comeback was a resounding success, as the young right-hander went 16–4. The Orioles offense slugged 175 home runs, led by Boog Powell's 37 home runs and 121 RBIs, and Frank Robinson had 32 home runs and 100 RBIs. They had four other players in double digits for home runs, including a career high 26 for Paul Blair. They drew 1,058,168 fans to Memorial Stadium, the sixth time the club had gone over a million in attendance.

Now they would face the Minnesota Twins in the first AL Championship Series, and they would make short work of the Twins in the five-game series, although it would be close work. The Orioles won the first game in Baltimore, 4–3, in the twelfth inning on a squeeze bunt by Blair before a crowd of 43,000, with Powell, Belanger, and Frank Robinson all hitting home runs. They won Game 2 in extra innings as well—a 1–0 complete Game 3 hit masterpiece by McNally. It was a pinch-hit RBI single by Curt Motton in the eleventh inning that drove in Powell and won the game. The clincher wasn't as close, an 11–2 beating, as Blair had five hits, and Don Buford, who had emerged as a key player for the Orioles since coming over from the White Sox, had four hits.

Meanwhile, over in the National League, something very strange had been going on in the year that a man walked on the moon. The

New York Mets—the lovable losers of baseball—had gone from laughingstocks to the winners of the National League East, stunning the powerful Chicago Cubs. The Mets won 100 games with great young pitching, led by one of the greatest pitchers of his time, Tom Seaver, who was the NL Cy Young Award winner, with a 25–7 record, 208 strikeouts, and a 2.21 ERA; Jerry Koosman, who went 17–9 with a 2.28 ERA; and Gary Gentry, who had a 13–12 record and a 3.42 ERA. They also had a young fireballer who had posted a 6–3 record in 25 games, 10 of them starts, striking out 92 batters in 89 innings—Nolan Ryan.

Most of all, though, the mentality of the Mets was changed by a former favorite son of Brooklyn—former Dodgers first baseman Gil Hodges, who was the guiding force behind this mixture of talented young pitching and timely, if not powerful, hitting. The Mets hit just 109 home runs, led by Tommie Agee with 26, followed by Art Shamsky with 14 as a part-time player. They got an infusion of power when they traded for first baseman Donn Clendenon, who hit 12 home runs and drove in 37 runs in 72 games. And they also had the third-leading hitter in the National League that season, as left fielder Cleon Jones hit .340. But they were also surrounded in the lineup by a series of banjo hitters—Bud Harrelson, Ken Boswell, Rod Gaspar, and a familiar name to the Orioles, Al Weis.

The Mets had an easier time than the Orioles in their League Championship Series debut against the Atlanta Braves. They swept the Braves in three straight, none of them close—9–5 and 11–6 in Atlanta and 7–4 in the clincher at Shea Stadium, which was torn apart by delirious Mets fans celebrating the pennant victory.

Still, despite winning 100 games and easily handling the Braves, the 1969 World Series was considered a mismatch by most observers because of the dominance of the Orioles that year and their All-Star talent on the mound and in the field. The Orioles were among those observers who believed it was a mismatch. Some of the players had watched the Mets clinch the pennant on a clubhouse television while they were finishing off the Twins. As the Orioles celebrated their own win, Frank Robinson was overheard by reporters as he shouted, "Bring on Ron Gaspar."

"*Rod*, stupid," Merv Rettenmund corrected Robinson, to which Robinson replied, "Bring on Rod Stupid."

But there were signs that this New York team should not be taken lightly by anyone associated with the city of Baltimore—that there were even forces of nature at work beyond the playing field. The New York Jets had already scored one of the greatest upsets in

The 1969 Orioles won 109 games, the most in franchise history. The anchor of the pitching staff, and the co-Cy Young winner that year, was Mike Cuellar, here delivering a pitch in Game 1 of the 1969 World Series.

12—Gold Glove Winners

Player	Number of Awards
Brooks Robinson	16
Mark Belanger	8
Paul Blair	8
Jim Palmer	4
Mike Mussina	4
Bobby Grich	4
Eddie Murray	3
Davey Johnson	3
Luis Aparicio	2
Cal Ripken	2
Rafael Palmeiro	2
Roberto Alomar	2

professional football history by defeating the heavily favored Baltimore Colts in January 1969 in Super Bowl III. Several months later, the New York Knicks upset the first-place Baltimore Bullets in the NBA playoffs. And don't forget—a man had walked on the moon.

Still, there was no reason to believe this World Series wouldn't play out as expected after Game 1 at Memorial Stadium before a crowd of 50,429. The Orioles were not impressed with Tom Terrific, as Buford led off the bottom of the first with a solo home run. He also hit a run-scoring double in the fourth inning, and the Mets did not score until the seventh inning in a 4–1 win by Cuellar, putting the Orioles on top, 1–0 in the Series. It was the first game Seaver had lost since early August.

Koosman, the left-hander, proved tougher for the Orioles lineup. Baltimore batters didn't even get a hit off Koosman until the seventh inning. The Mets led at the time, 1–0, thanks to a fourth-inning home run by Clendenon off McNally, the only run McNally would give up in eight innings. But Blair singled in the seventh, stole second, and came around to score on a Brooks Robinson single to tie the game at 1–1. New York would even the Series in the ninth inning when, with two outs, Ed Charles singled past Brooks Robinson and went to third on a single by Jerry Grote. Al Weis—the same Al Weis who had taken Frank Robinson out two years before—was the next hitter, and he singled in the winning run for a 2–1 Mets victory to tie the Series, one game apiece.

Palmer started Game 3 for the Orioles, with the Series moving to Shea Stadium, and Agee, like Buford did in Game 1, led off in the bottom of the first for the Mets with a home run for a 1–0 New York lead. Gary Gentry, the Mets starter, would help his own cause with a two-run double in the second inning, increasing New York's lead to 3–0. Gentry had driven in just one run all season long.

Agee would star in the game with his glove as well; with two outs and two Orioles runners on base in the fourth, Agee ran down a shot by Elrod Hendricks, snaring the ball in the web of his glove—the proverbial "ice cream cone"—before crashing into the wall. He would do it again in the seventh inning, when Mets starter Gary Gentry loaded the bases. Blair hit a blast into the right-center-field alley off reliever Nolan Ryan that had all the earmarks of a bases-clearing triple. But Agee dove headfirst and snared it, his body sliding about 15 feet while he held onto the ball. Ed Kranepool added an eighth-inning home run, and the Mets prevailed, 5–0.

Game 4 would take place on the same day that the country was engaged in a symbolic event that would illustrate the turmoil of the times—Moratorium Day, when people were supposed to stop what they were doing to protest the Vietnam War. It also illustrated how the Mets had captured the attention of the country. They were a Cinderella story in very dark times.

Seaver took the mound against Cuellar, and Clendenon continued the trend of the Series by staking his pitching to a quick lead with a solo home run in the bottom of the second, putting New York on top, 1–0. In a pitching duel, it stayed that way until the ninth inning, when, with Frank Robinson on third base, Brooks Robinson hit a sinking line drive to right field that would propel Ron Swoboda into World Series history. Swoboda, who was born and raised in Baltimore, took off to try to catch a ball that he appeared

TRIVIA

Who was the first Orioles pitcher to win the Cy Young Award?

Answers to the trivia questions are on pages 165–166.

to have no shot at. But he dove headfirst, stretched out as far as he could, and caught the ball just before it hit the ground, in what is still considered to be the greatest catch in World Series history. Frank Robinson scored on the sacrifice, and the game was tied 1–1. The Mets magic was just getting started, though. In the bottom of the tenth, Grote led off with a double that dropped in front of Buford in left field. "Who's Rod Gaspar?" came in to run for Grote. The Orioles intentionally walked Weis, and then Hodges sent J. C. Martin up as a pinch-hitter to bunt Gaspar over to third. Martin got the bunt down, but when pitcher Pete Richert tried to throw him out at first base, the ball hit Martin on his left wrist and went off toward second base. Gaspar came around to score for a 2–1 Mets win, leaving them just one game away from being World Series champions.

McNally started Game 5, and as he had done before, helped himself at the plate with a two-run home run off Koosman in the third inning. Frank Robinson followed with a solo home run, and the Orioles appeared to be on the verge of holding off elimination with a 3–0 lead. But in the bottom of the sixth, Cleon Jones moved away from the plate, claiming he was hit on the foot by a pitch. Umpire Lou DiMuro disagreed, and ordered him back into the box. When Hodges came out to argue, he pointed out that there was shoe polish on the ball, so DiMuro sent Jones to first. Clendenon then hit his third home run of the Series to cut the Orioles lead to 3–2. Weis, of all people, tied it in the bottom of the seventh with a solo home run. The Mets won it in the bottom of the eighth on an RBI single by Swoboda, and a ground ball by Grote that brought Swoboda in for a 5–3 win before a crazed crowd of 57,000 and a group of stunned Orioles players who were convinced that they were the best team in baseball, which made the Series loss all the more difficult to swallow.

They never did swallow it. The Orioles would carry that loss throughout the entire off-season and into spring training for the 1970 season. It would become their rallying cry.

Frank Robinson

In spring training in 1966, a young Baltimore Orioles pitcher named Jim Palmer sat in the dugout as his new teammate Frank Robinson got up to hit for the first time as an Oriole. He drilled a line drive, and did so impressively enough that Palmer turned to one of his teammates and declared that he believed they had just won the pennant.

He was right.

The Orioles were building something impressive in the early 1960s with a farm development system that produced such young stars as Paul Blair, Boog Powell, and Davey Johnson, and a pitching staff that included Dave McNally and a young Palmer. And they already had a star presence in Brooks Robinson, the perennial All-Star third baseman who had won the American League Most Valuable Player honor in 1964.

But the arrival of Frank Robinson in 1966 changed the personality of the franchise from competitive to dominant. And though the franchise would stay competitive until its last World Series appearance in 1983 because of its standout player development system, it would never dominate baseball as the Orioles did during Frank Robinson's tenure in Baltimore, from 1966 to 1971. These are just six years of a 21-season Hall of Fame career, but they are the ones that Robinson is most closely identified with.

During those six years, the Orioles went to the World Series four times—1966 against the Los Angeles Dodgers, 1969 against the New York Mets, 1970 against the Cincinnati Reds, and 1971 against the Pittsburgh Pirates. They won two of them, beating the Dodgers in four straight games in 1966 and the Reds in five games in 1970. They would only reach the World Series two more times after Robinson left the franchise.

Robinson was already an established All-Star player when he came to Baltimore in 1966. He broke in with the Reds 10 years earlier and had already hit more than 300 home runs. He led Cincinnati to the National League pennant in 1961, when he hit 37 home runs, drove in 124 runs, and batted .323. Robinson followed that up with better numbers in 1962, slugging 39 home runs, driving in 136 runs, and batting .342. And he had the reputation of being perhaps the toughest player in baseball, standing in the box and taking the best shots of such intimidating pitchers as Don Drysdale and Bob Gibson, and usually leading the league in getting hit by pitchers, eventually being plunked 198 times over his career.

"He played harder than most—not really dirty, just very aggressive," said Don Zimmer, a Reds teammate in 1962. "I came to respect that, even appreciate it, as his teammate. But as an opponent, that was another story. You respected him, only grudgingly."

However, despite the fact that Robinson hit 33 home runs and drove in 113 runs in 1965, Reds general manager Bill DeWitt traded

Outfielder Frank Robinson won the American League MVP in 1966, the year he was traded to the Orioles from Cincinnati, where he had won a National League MVP.

him in December 1965 to the Orioles for pitchers Milt Pappas and Jack Baldschun and outfielder Dick Simpson. DeWitt declared he felt Robinson's best days were behind him. "Robinson is not a young 30," he told reporters at the time. "If he had been 26, we might not have traded him."

It was a terrible miscalculation. Robinson was far from done. He turned in the best season of his career in Baltimore in 1966, blasting 49 home runs, driving in 122 runs, scoring 122 runs, and batting .316—not just winning the American League MVP honors, but also the Triple Crown, leading the league in home runs, RBIs, and batting average. He proved Bill DeWitt wrong.

What award did Frank Robinson receive in 1958?

Answers to the trivia questions are on pages 165–166.

"He never played like someone with a chip on his shoulder, although he had a right to feel disrespected," Brooks Robinson said. "Instead, he took it as a challenge to make [the Reds] regret losing him. In a big way, they did us a favor."

Yes, they did. Robinson became the leader of the team, setting the tone in the clubhouse and on the field for professionalism and winning baseball games. The mentality he describes in his book, *My Life Is Baseball,* after the Orioles upset the defending World Series champion Dodgers in the 1966 World Series, is the personality the Orioles took on after he arrived. "There was never any doubt in my mind we would beat them," Robinson wrote. "I think it just proves that if you're dedicated to a cause, if you want something badly enough, you can really do it."

Robinson never approached those numbers again, though he continued to be a productive hitter and the leader of the team, hitting 30 home runs and driving in 94 runs in 1967, and then, struggling with injuries, hitting just 15 home runs and driving in only 52 runs in 421 at-bats in 1968. But he bounced back in 1969 with 32 home runs and 100 RBIs, and led the Orioles back to the World Series—where they got embarrassed by the Miracle Mets in five games.

He brought the team back to the Series in 1970, when they defeated his former team, the Reds, in five games, and then made

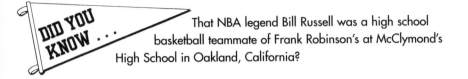

That NBA legend Bill Russell was a high school basketball teammate of Frank Robinson's at McClymond's High School in Oakland, California?

one final World Series journey, losing to the Pirates and Roberto Clemente in 1971.

Along the way, he also began laying the groundwork for what would be his historic life after baseball—that of a manager. In 1968, he took advantage of an opportunity to manage in Puerto Rico. Earl Weaver had been managing there during the winter, but after getting the job in Baltimore, he had to discontinue his position there. Robinson heard about it and asked if he could be considered for the job. He was hired, and gained the valuable experience he would need to achieve his goal of managing in the major leagues—something no black man had ever done before.

After the 1971 season, Robinson was stunned once more when he was traded by the Orioles to the Dodgers for pitchers Doyle Alexander and Bob O'Brien, outfielder Royle Stillman, and catcher Sergio Robles—perhaps as bad a trade as the one made to bring Robinson to Baltimore.

He wasn't the only one who was stunned. "He taught us how to win," Davey Johnson said. And Weaver was quoted as saying, "I'm scared to death giving up Frank."

Robinson said he was hurt by the deal. "You think you were an important part of the club," he said. "You contributed a lot to them. Then suddenly you feel like they think they don't need you anymore. They've got somebody better to take your place. Your feelings are hurt, your pride is hurt."

Robinson played in just 103 games for the Dodgers in 1972, with 19 home runs and 59 RBIs. But he was traded back to the American League to the California Angels, where, at the age of 37, he could take advantage of the new designated-hitter position. He hit 30 home runs and drove in 97 runs in 1973 for the Angels—his last hurrah as a player. He split time between the Angels and the Cleveland Indians in 1974, and then made history when the Indians named him player/manager, making him the first black manager in Major

League Baseball. Robinson said at a news conference, "I'm the first black manager only because I was born black."

He would see brief playing time the next two years as a player/manager before retiring for good as a player after the 1976 season. When he did, Robinson was fourth in baseball history in home runs with 586, 1,812 RBIs, 2,943 hits, and a .294 batting average.

Robinson came in one game under .500 in Cleveland his first year, with a 79–80 record—a success by the dismal Indians standards, and then turned in an 81–78 winning season. But after a 26–31 start in 1977, Robinson was fired. He returned to the Orioles organization for one year, managing their Class AAA Rochester team, and then was hired to manage the San Francisco Giants. He managed four seasons there, losing the division title to the rival Dodgers on the last day of the season in 1982, and was fired in August 1984.

Robinson returned to Baltimore on the coaching staff and then was hired to manage the club in 1988, and won AL Manager of the Year honors in 1989, taking a mediocre Orioles team to the brink of the division title in a battle with the Blue Jays. After stepping down in 1991, he stayed with the organization as an assistant general manager until 1995. After that, Robinson would work in baseball in various roles, including being in charge of on-field discipline, before being asked to manage the Montreal Expos in 2002 when baseball took over the franchise. After the team was relocated to Washington in 2005, Robinson received an honor worthy of his resume—the Presidential Medal of Freedom, honoring him for his role as a pioneer for blacks in baseball.

There are six numbers retired by the Baltimore Orioles, and most of those historic figures—Jim Palmer, Brooks Robinson, and Eddie Murray among them—spent their entire career, or a majority of it, in an Orioles uniform. Robinson spent only six years, but left a legacy as large as any in team history.

Taking Care of Business

Losing to the Mets in the 1969 World Series was never far from the minds of the Baltimore Orioles during the winter that followed, and it would be one of the primary motivations for this club going into the 1970 season. The group of players that had started with the 1966 World Series win over the Los Angeles Dodgers felt they should have more to show for their talent than that one World Series championship. No team in the American League in the 1960s—not the Yankees, the Tigers, or the Twins—had won more games than the Baltimore Orioles.

Remarkably, they struggled in spring training, going 11–12, but in reality this was a team that was ready to play when they arrived in Miami. The exhibition games were just a matter of passing time until they got to the business at hand when the regular season began—winning the American League pennant and getting back to the World Series.

"I think this ballclub is probably the best ballclub I've ever been on," said longtime Orioles coach Billy Hunter before the season started. "I think I made that statement last year and really it is probably more accurate this year than it was last year, because our bench is a little stronger and for all-around, a 25-guy unit, this is the best I have ever seen."

The Orioles business would differ from the business of baseball that captured the headlines in 1970. The spotlight would be off the field, as baseball was caught in the midst of change that gripped American society as the 1960s came to an end. First there was former 30-game winner Denny McLain, who was suspended for consorting with gamblers and missed half of the season. Then there was

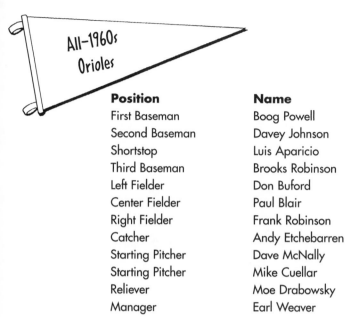

All–1960s
Orioles

Position	Name
First Baseman	Boog Powell
Second Baseman	Davey Johnson
Shortstop	Luis Aparicio
Third Baseman	Brooks Robinson
Left Fielder	Don Buford
Center Fielder	Paul Blair
Right Fielder	Frank Robinson
Catcher	Andy Etchebarren
Starting Pitcher	Dave McNally
Starting Pitcher	Mike Cuellar
Reliever	Moe Drabowsky
Manager	Earl Weaver

outfielder Curt Flood, who was fighting his historic court battle against baseball's reserve clause after being traded from the St. Louis Cardinals to the Philadelphia Phillies. He sat out the season and filed an antitrust lawsuit. Finally, the curtain of baseball innocence was pulled back when Jim Bouton's tell-all book, *Ball Four,* hit the bookstores and caused a furor.

In Baltimore, though, time had stood still after the disappointment of the 1969 World Series. There was only baseball, and returning to the World Series.

The Orioles got off to a quick start, sweeping the Indians in three games in Cleveland to open the season, then coming home to Baltimore to win the home opener, 3–2 over the Tigers. They were 5–0 in the first five games, then went 5–5 over the next 10 before taking off and leaving the field behind.

One of the key players in Baltimore's success in 1969 and 1970 was the scrappy outfielder they got from the White Sox in 1968, Don Buford. He had won a World Series playing for USC in college, and he arrived in Baltimore with the hope of winning one as a major leaguer as well. He opened the season in 1970 as if he were on a one-man mission to accomplish that goal.

Dave McNally, here in 1971, won 20 games four straight years (1968–1971) for the Orioles.

In an April 9, 1970, contest against the Cleveland Indians, Buford hit home runs from both sides of the plate in a 13–1 win, becoming the first Orioles player to clear the fences as a switch-hitter in one game. More than two weeks later, Buford—not a home-run hitter— blasted a three-run home run to give the Orioles a 10–9 win over Kansas City. The home run was, in some ways, the shot that clinched the pennant. With the victory, Baltimore took over first place and would not lose it for the rest of the season.

They stayed in first place in part because they were more than just a two-man team of Frank and Brooks Robinson. They were gaining power up and down the lineup. On April 29, they showed that diversified power in an 18–2 beating of the Chicago White Sox. Powell homered and so did Hendricks, but Blair led the offense with three home runs and six RBIs.

It was a devastating combination—the big bats and the All-Star pitching rotation of McNally, Palmer, and Cuellar, who continued to dominate the rest of the league. On May 29, Cuellar struck out four consecutive batters in the fourth inning of a 2–0 shutout win over the California Angels. He allowed just four hits, while Powell's two-run home run was more than Cuellar would need. Everything was rolling along just fine until two days later, in the series finale against the Angels, when the Orioles would be dealt a serious blow.

In the eighth inning of their May 31 game against the Angels, California pitcher Ken Tatum hit Powell with a pitch. Then he hit Blair in the face with a pitch that broke Blair's nose and several bones in his face. They had to bring a stretcher out onto the field to carry Blair off. Baltimore would lose the game, 6–1. Blair would be out for several weeks and return, but he would never be the same player. He would go from a career high of 26 home runs, 76 RBIs, 102 runs scored, and a .285 average in 1969 to 18 home runs, 65 RBIs, 79 runs scored, and a .267 average in 1970 down to 10 home runs, 44 RBIs, 75 runs scored, and a .262 average in 1971.

While the team was on a collective mission, there were individual goals realized during the season. Brooks Robinson would reach a milestone on June 20 against Joe Coleman and the Washington Senators when he hit a three-run home run in the fifth inning to help the Orioles to a 5–4 win. It was his 2,000th career hit.

One-run wins were not unusual for the Orioles in 1970. When the season was over, Baltimore would have won 40 of the 55 one-run games they played. But they won all kinds of games in all sorts of ways. On June 25, they were losing to the Red Sox 7–0 at Fenway Park after five innings, but came back to tie the game at 7–7 in the top of the ninth inning on a Merv Rettenmund home run and a double by Etchebarren. This would not be a one-run game, though. Baltimore scored six runs in the fourteenth inning for a 13–7 win.

The next day in Washington, they won another way. Frank Robinson hit two consecutive grand-slam home runs in a 12–2 victory over the Senators, just the seventh major league player to ever accomplish that slugging feat. Each time, the same three runners crossed the plate ahead of Frank Robinson—

TRIVIA

Who was on the cover of the 1970 Orioles Yearbook?

Answers to the trivia questions are on pages 165–166.

Frank Robinson, who managed the Washington Nationals in their first two years in the nation's capital, hit the last grand slam at RFK Stadium before the Senators left for Arlington, Texas, after the 1971 season. On June 26, 1970, Robinson became the seventh player to hit two grand slams in one game, and, like former Oriole Jim Gentile, he did it in consecutive innings, the first one coming against Joe Coleman and the second against Joe Grzenda. Robinson was manager when Brad Wilkerson hit the next grand slam at RFK in 2005.

McNally (the winning pitcher), Buford, and Blair. Those would be the only grand slams Frank Robinson would hit during his six years as an Oriole. The second one would be the last grand slam hit at RFK Stadium for 35 years. The Senators would leave Washington after the 1971 season, moving to Arlington, Texas, to become the Texas Rangers, and baseball would not return to the nation's capital until the Montreal Expos relocated and became the Washington Nationals in 2005. On August 4, 2005, Nationals outfielder Brad Wilkerson became the first player since Frank Robinson to hit a grand slam at RFK Stadium. Ironically, Frank Robinson was there to see it, as manager of the Nationals.

Less than two weeks later, Brooks Robinson delivered his own grand theatrics with a tenth-inning grand-slam home run off New York Yankees pitcher Lindy McDaniel to break a 2–2 tie and give Baltimore a 6–2 victory. One day later, the Orioles, down 8–6 to the Yankees, who had been coming on the AL East, came back to win 9–8 on Frank Robinson's home run and a two-out single by Buford—also coming off Lindy McDaniel. Looking back, Buford, who had fouled off five pitches before making contact, believes it was one of the more important games of the 1970 season. "They had been gaining ground on us, and that was a key part of the season," Buford said.

Baltimore went into the All-Star break with a 54–33 record. Eight Orioles—Frank Robinson, Brooks Robinson, Johnson, Powell, Palmer, McNally, Cuellar, and manager Earl Weaver—were all members of the AL squad. Palmer started the game and pitched three shutout innings, but the AL lost to the NL 5–4 in 12 innings at

Cincinnati's new ballpark, Riverfront Stadium—a ballpark the Orioles would be revisiting before the year was over.

The Orioles picked up where they left off after the first half of the season. Buford delivered another game-winning home run in a 6–5 win over the Twins in a game that saw Orioles reliever Dick Hall get a hit, his first of the year, and defeat Minnesota's Tom Hall on July 25. The next day, the meat of the order, Powell, drove in six runs, with a bases-loaded single and a grand-slam home run, for an 11–1 win over the Twins. Powell would have a career year, hitting 35 home runs, driving in 114 runs, and batting .297 on his way to the AL Most Valuable Player award. But going into the second half, the Orioles were focused on just one award—a World Series championship.

Pedal to the Metal

The Orioles played like an All-Star team, with outstanding pitching and hitting the second half of the 1970 season. Dave McNally won his 20th game on August 25 in a 5–1 win over the Oakland A's, even though the Athletics got 10 hits off McNally. Two days later, Mike Cuellar won his 20th, a 6–4 victory over the A's. On September 20, Jim Palmer won his 20th, a 7–0 shutout over the Indians, making the Orioles the first team in 14 years to have three 20-game winners.

The Orioles stepped on the gas hard at the end, winning their last 11 consecutive games, finishing with a 3–2 win over the Senators at Memorial Stadium, as Frank Robinson hit his 475th career home run, tying him for 12th on the all-time list with Stan Musial. Baltimore finished the regular season with a 108–54 record, 15 games ahead of second-place New York. Over a two-year period, the Orioles had won 217 games, a league record.

They would face the Twins again in the AL Championship Series, and it would be a repeat of their 1969 three-game sweep of Minnesota. Baltimore won the series opener in Minnesota on October 3 before a crowd of 39,324 by the score of 10–6. Cuellar, the winning pitcher, delivered the big blow, the team's signature hit that year—a grand-slam home run in the seven-run fourth inning. The next day Johnson and Frank Robinson homered to lead Baltimore to an 11–3 win, and again, a pitcher—this one McNally—proved his worth at the plate with a double. Palmer clinched it with a 6–1 victory in Game 3 at Memorial Stadium.

Over in the National League, the Big Red Machine in Cincinnati had walked through its competition with nearly identical dominance, with a 102–60 record, finishing 14½ games ahead of the

Dodgers in the NL West. Playing in a new ballpark along the Ohio River, with a new manager named George "Sparky" Anderson, this was the start of the Big Red Machine that would be the premier team in the NL in the 1970s. It was led by one of the greatest catchers of all time, Johnny Bench, who was the NL Most Valuable Player, with 45 home runs, 148 RBIs, and a .293 average; the man who would eventually have more hits than anyone who ever played the game—and then be banned from the game for gambling as the Reds manager—Pete Rose, who scored 120 runs with 205 hits and a .316 average; future Hall of Famer Tony Perez, who slugged 40 home runs, drove

The Orioles won the 1970 World Series against the Reds for their second championship in five years. Catcher Elrod Hendricks contributed to the cause with this double in Game 5, won 6–5 by the Orioles.

IF ONLY . . . The Hall of Fame had kept Brooks Robinson's glove, he might have not won five of his Gold Gloves. The glove that Brooks Robinson used for his legendary fielding exploits in the 1970 World Series was a hand-me-down from former Oriole Dave May. After the Series, the glove was sent to Cooperstown for display in the National Baseball Hall of Fame, but Robinson asked for it back for the 1971 season because he couldn't find a replacement to his liking.

in 129 runs, and batted .317; and Lee May, who slammed 34 home runs and drove in 94 runs. With 191 home runs and 726 RBIs, it was a lineup that was equal to the Orioles offense of 179 home runs and 748 RBIs. They fell short in the pitching matchups, though. The rotation of Jim Merritt (20–12), Gary Nolan (18–7), Wayne Simpson (14–3), and Jim McGlothlin (14–10) was solid, but Simpson would be sidelined for the World Series with a shoulder injury and Merritt would be limited by a sore elbow.

Like the Orioles, the Reds dispatched their opponent in the NL championship series, the Pirates, in three games—all done through outstanding pitching performances. Nolan and Clay Carroll combined on a 3–0 shutout in Game 1 on October 3 in Pittsburgh, and Merritt, with Carroll and a young Don Gullet in relief, allowed one run in a 3–1 Reds victory in Game 2. Pirates hitters made progress in Game 3, scoring two runs off the Reds pitching, but Cincinnati scored three runs for the third straight game in a 3–2 clinching victory. Now the Reds would welcome the Orioles—a team on a mission ever since Cleon Jones caught the final out for the Mets in the 1969 World Series—for the 1970 Fall Classic in their new home.

But when the Series was over, Riverfront Stadium and all of baseball would belong to Brooks Robinson.

After the Jackson Five sang the National Anthem to kick off the Series, the Reds took a 3–0 lead before a crowd of 51,531 on Lee May's two-run home run, but the Orioles, as they had so many times during the season, came back to win a one-run game 4–3, behind Palmer (who had just come off clinching the ALCS against the Twins) on the mound and home runs by Boog Powell, Elrod Hendricks, and Brooks Robinson. But the play that showed that 1970 would not be a repeat of 1969 was one where the Orioles got the benefit of a controversial call. In the sixth inning, with one out, Bernie Carbo on third base and Tommy Helms at first, Reds pinch-hitter Ty Cline hit a high chopper in front of the plate. Home-plate umpire Ken Burkhart called it a fair ball. Hendricks, behind the plate for Baltimore, fielded the ball, and, instead of going to first base, turned around and tried to tag Carbo out as he was coming home. They ran into each other, and Burkhart called Carbo out. But replays showed that Hendricks had the ball in his right hand and tagged Carbo with his empty glove hand.

It might have been the play the 1970 World Series would be known for, but Brooks Robinson made any sour grapes seem unreasonable with his dazzling play at third base on the ballpark's artificial surface, and it started in that same inning in Game 1. May led off the sixth inning for Cincinnati by hitting a shot between Brooks Robinson and third base. Brooks Robinson moved quickly and backhanded the ball when it was past him and, while moving toward foul territory, turned and threw out May. It is a play that has been repeated in highlights over and over again.

Game 2 in Cincinnati started like a repeat of Game 1. The Reds grabbed a 3–0 lead, but Powell's fourth inning home run and then a two-run double by Hendricks led the Orioles back to another one-run win, 6–5. Tom Phoebus, in relief, got the win for Baltimore.

The Series moved back to Baltimore and Memorial Stadium for Game 3, with 51,773 showing up to watch McNally. Rose and Nolan led off with back-to-back hits, but Brooks Robinson continued his Series show, this time for the hometown fans, when he made a leaping catch of Perez's sharp grounder, got up, stepped on third, and threw to first to nail the double player. Brooks Robinson gave Baltimore a 2–0 lead in the bottom of the first with a two-run double. Then, in the second inning, he ran down Helms's slow roller and threw him out at first. Then he made another remarkable diving catch on a bench line drive in the sixth inning, as a nationwide audience learned what Orioles fans had known for

TRIVIA

Who dubbed Brooks Robinson the "Human Vacuum Cleaner"?

Answers to the trivia questions are on pages 165–166.

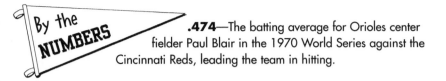

many years—that Brooks Robinson was the greatest player to take the position at third base the game had ever seen.

This time, though, the Orioles win would not be a one-run affair. This was a 9–3 beating, with the big hit by a pitcher—hardly unusual for the Orioles—as McNally hammered, of course, a grand-slam home run, the only one by a pitcher in the history of the World Series.

Because Simpson was available for duty, and Merritt had a tender elbow, Anderson was forced to start Nolan again for Game 4 against Palmer, and he didn't last long, just 2⅔ innings. But May saved the day for the Reds when, down 5–3 in the top of the eighth, he slammed a three-run home run off reliever Eddie Watt; the Reds would win this one-run game by the score of 6–5. But the win just saved the Reds the embarrassment of being swept.

In Game 5 at Memorial Stadium, in front of 45,341, the Reds hit Cuellar hard in the top of the first, with four hits and three runs. But Merritt, taking the mound with his sore elbow, didn't make it past the second inning. The Orioles scored two runs in the first, second, and third innings, and would coast to a 9–3 win behind home runs by Frank Robinson and Merv Rettemund, and eight innings of shutout ball by Cuellar after his first-inning setback. The Baltimore Orioles had claimed the title they believed had been theirs the year before—World Series champions, their second such championship in five years. Brooks Robinson would be named Most Valuable Player for his standard-setting play at third base.

After the game, in the clubhouse celebration, Frank Robinson reaffirmed their motivation for 1970—the loss to the Mets the year before. "We were reflecting on 1969 all this year, although no one would come out and say it," he said. "We dedicated ourselves since spring training to win the American League championship this year and come out on top in the World Series."

Brooks Robinson went out of his way to praise his teammate, Frank Robinson, for the run that began in 1966. "I tell you, getting Frank Robinson in 1966 really put us over the top," he said. "We were a good ballclub, and that made us the best around for a while."

But this 1970 World Series had been the Brooks Robinson show. Lee May dubbed him with the nickname that would stick when he commented after that game about the third baseman's glove work. "Man, that guy is like a human vacuum cleaner down there," May said.

They would get one more opportunity to show how great this Orioles squad would be the following year—their last chance.

The Final Run

Orioles general manager Harry Dalton didn't rest on the laurels of the World Series championship his team had just won. He had arguably the best team in baseball over the past two years, but he would work to make them even stronger. On December 1, 1970, Dalton traded pitchers Tom Phoebus, Al Severinsen, and Fred Beene and shortstop Enzo Hernandez to the San Diego Padres for pitchers Pat Dobson and Tom Dukes. The deal would be reminiscent of the one they made to get Cuellar, though not paying off for nearly as long. Like Cuellar, Dobson was coming off a losing season, going 14–15 for the Padres. And, like Cuellar, he would come to Baltimore and, under pitching coach George Bamberger, win 20 games for the Orioles in 1971.

That would be good enough for fourth in Baltimore's historic 1971 pitching rotation.

Baltimore opened up the season with a 3–2 win at home against the Washington Senators, their traditional I-95 opponent—the last Opening Day against the Senators, who would leave Washington after the season and move to Arlington, Texas, to become the Texas Rangers.

The Orioles took early control of the AL East with an 8–2 record in their first 10 games of the 1971 season. Then they struggled, going 18–17 until the end of May, when they took off on a nine-game winning streak and did not look back again the rest of the season. The starters all went on different hot streaks—Cuellar winning 11 straight, followed by Dobson with a 12-game winning streak. McNally would win 13 straight games over three months, despite missing four weeks with elbow problems. Both Cuellar and Palmer

70

would make the AL All-Star team, as did Frank and Brooks Robinson, with the squad managed again by Weaver. In a memorable game on July 13 in Detroit, the AL finally won a game 6–4—the only All-Star game the league would win between 1962 and 1983. Roberto Clemente, Hank Aaron, and Bench would homer for the NL, while Harmon Killebrew, Reggie Jackson, and Frank Robinson hit home runs to lead the AL. Jackson's home run traveled 520 feet. Frank Robinson's two-run home run was the game winner—and also the first time a player hit All-Star home runs in both leagues—and good enough for him to win Most Valuable Player honors.

As the Orioles rolled through the rest of the 1971 season, there were mostly good days with a few bad ones mixed in, such as July 28,

Jim Palmer, here pitching to Roberto Clemente in Game 6 of the 1971 World Series, won one game in the series, which the Orioles lost in seven to the Pirates.

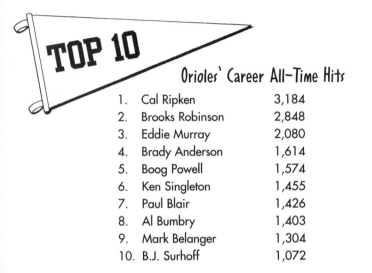

Orioles' Career All-Time Hits

1. Cal Ripken   3,184
2. Brooks Robinson 2,848
3. Eddie Murray   2,080
4. Brady Anderson   1,614
5. Boog Powell   1,574
6. Ken Singleton   1,455
7. Paul Blair   1,426
8. Al Bumbry   1,403
9. Mark Belanger   1,304
10. B.J. Surhoff   1,072

when Brooks Robinson had the worst day in the field in his career. He committed three errors in one inning against the Oakland Athletics.

Harmon Killebrew became the 10th player in baseball history to reach 500 home runs, hitting two to get 501 on August 10 against Baltimore, but the Orioles still won with Cuellar on the mound by a score of 4–3.

More than a month later, on September 13, Frank Robinson homered in each game of a doubleheader split with the Tigers, becoming the 11th member of the 500-home-runs club with his second blast. Then the parade of pitching history began. Dave McNally shut out the Yankees 5–0 on September 21 for his 20th victory, the fourth straight 20-win season for McNally. Then, three days later, Cuellar won his 20th, a 9–2 win over the Indians in the first game of a doubleheader to clinch the AL East for Baltimore. In the second game, Dobson hurled a 7–0 shutout to record his 20th victory. Two days after that, Palmer also shut out Cleveland by the score of 5–0 for his 20th win, becoming the Orioles' fourth 20-game winner. Only one other team in major league history—the 1920 Chicago White Sox—had four 20-game-winners on its staff.

The Orioles would finish the season with a record of 101–57, 12 games ahead of second-place Detroit. While the pitching staff put up nearly unprecedented numbers, the offense was not as strong as it had been in the past. Powell missed 30 games with injuries, but still hit 22 home runs and drove in 92 runs. Frank Robinson hit 28 home runs and had 99 RBIs, while Brooks Robinson slugged 20 home runs and drove in 92 runs.

Unlike the previous two AL Championship Series, the Orioles would not face the Twins this time. Instead, they would go up against a young, talented Oakland Athletics squad, winners of the AL West with a record of 101–60, finishing 16 games ahead of the second-place Kansas City Royals. The A's were led by flamboyant slugger Reggie Jackson and a 21-year-old left-hander named Vida Blue, who posted a 24–8 record and captured not only the AL Cy Young Award, but Most Valuable Player honors as well. This was the future of the American League, and they would prove to be a nemesis for Baltimore. But not this year.

The Orioles swept the ALCS for the third straight year, which meant that they had not lost a series game since the intra-league series began in 1969. Led by McNally on the mound and Blair's two-run double, the Orioles scored four runs in the seventh inning to win Game 1 on October 3 at Memorial Stadium, 5–3, before a crowd of 42,621. They beat the A's again 5–1 the next day. Four of the seven hits Baltimore batters got off Oakland starter Catfish Hunter were home runs—two home runs by Powell and home runs by Hendricks and Brooks Robinson. Cuellar got the complete-game victory before a surprisingly small crowd of 35,003. Postseason play had become commonplace for baseball fans in Baltimore.

Game 3 would take place in Oakland on October 5, and Palmer got the complete-game win in the series finale, 5–3—their first post-season game in Oakland, which drew 33,176.

In the National League, the Pittsburgh Pirates, who had lost the year before to the Reds in the NLCS, won the East division for the second straight year. They were led by slugger Willie Stargell, their left fielder, who blasted 48 home runs and drove in 125 runs, and the great Roberto Clemente, who batted .341 and drove in 86 runs. Their ace was the psychedelic Dock Ellis, who had a 19–9 mark, followed by Steve Blass, who, before he got Steve Blass disease and could not find home plate anymore, posted a 15–8 record.

TRIVIA

Who was nicknamed "the Snake"?

Answers to the trivia questions are on pages 165–166.

The Pirates would move on to the World Series by beating the San Francisco Giants three games to one in the National League series.

Just as the 1970 World Series had proven to be a national showcase that would forever seal the legacy of Brooks Robinson, the 1971 Series would serve the same purpose for another player—Clemente. The Pirates outfielder stole the show with his dazzling glove, hot bat, and daring base running.

Baltimore won Game 1 at home on October 9 before a crowd of 53,229 by the score of 5–3, behind McNally's three-hitter and Merv Rettenmund's three-run home run. Frank Robinson also homered off Ellis, just like he did in the All-Star Game—the first time a batter had that combination of home runs. And the Orioles rolled to a Game 2 win before 53,239 fans at Memorial Stadium by an 11–3 margin, as Brooks Robinson tied a Series record by reaching base five straight times on three hits and two walks.

When the Series moved to Pittsburgh and another new artificial-turf ballpark, Three Rivers Stadium, the Pirates got the upper hand when Blass tossed a three-hitter in Game 3 on October 12 before 50,403 fans and Bob Robertson hit a three-run home run in a 5–1 victory. And Pittsburgh survived three runs from the Orioles in the first inning of Game 4 on October 13 to come back and win 4–3 to tie the Series at two games apiece, as Clemente went 3 for 4 before 51,378 fans in the first night Series game ever played. Nelson Briles, who made only 14 starts for the Pirates in 1971, got the start in Game 5 on October 14 in Pittsburgh before a crowd of 51,377 and threw a two-hitter, shutting out Baltimore 4–0.

The Orioles came back to tie the Series before 44,174 hometown fans in Game 6 when, with the score tied 2–2 in the bottom of the tenth inning, Frank Robinson walked, moved to third in an aggressive base-running move on Rettenmund's slow ground single up the middle, and scored the game-winning run on Brooks Robinson's shallow fly ball to center field. That set up Game 7. Of the three previous times the Orioles played in the World Series, none of them had gone past five games. This would be their first Game 7. The Orioles seemed to have everything going their way—playing at Memorial Stadium before 47,291 Orioles fans with Cuellar on the mound going against Blass. But Blass was up to the task. Pittsburgh took a 1–0 lead in the fourth inning on a Clemente home run, and then made it a 2–0 game on an RBI double by Jose Pagan in the eighth inning. Baltimore would manage to score one run in the bottom of the inning on an RBI grounder by Buford, but the Pirates would hang on for a 2–1 victory and the World Series championship.

Clemente was the toast of baseball. He batted .414 in the Series, with 12 hits in 29 at-bats, and was named Series MVP. Tragically, nearly 15 months later, Clemente died in a plane crash off the coast of his native Puerto Rico as he attempted to take food, clothing, and medical supplies to earthquake victims in Nicaragua.

Little did Orioles fans realize that the trips to the World Series that had become commonplace in Baltimore were almost over. They were about to witness the end of an era, an era in which the Orioles—over a six-year period—went to four World Series and won two of them.

If Orioles fans didn't realize it when the 1971 Series ended, they got the word on December 2, when Frank Robinson was traded with Pete Richert to the Los Angeles Dodgers for Doyle Alexander, Bob O'Brien, Sergio Robles, and Royle Stillman. Frank Robinson had only played six of his 21 major league seasons with the Orioles, but it would become the franchise he would be most identified with. He would come back to manage the team in the late 1980s and then serve as assistant general manager in the 1990s. "I had more team success in Baltimore and became more recognizable playing with the Orioles instead of the Reds," Frank Robinson said. "We won two world championships and four American League championships. It was about team success, not individual."

Life without Frank

With Frank Robinson's arrival, the team's success began. And there can be no denying that with his departure, the team's success ended, although the Orioles hardly collapsed. They were still the standard for Major League Baseball organizations, even though Dalton left after the 1971 season to run the Milwaukee Brewers for Bud Selig. Hoffberger's former right-hand man at the National Brewery, Frank Cashen—a former sportswriter who had been serving as the Orioles' executive vice president—took over as the Orioles' general manager for the 1972 season. The Orioles would finish third in the AL East with a record of 80–74, but they were just five games out of first place. Detroit barely won the division by a half game over the Boston Red Sox.

The Orioles would hit just 100 home runs, with Powell leading the team with 21 homers, followed by Bobby Grich with 12. Powell also led the team with just 81 RBIs. It was the pitching that carried the team. Palmer won 20 games for the third straight season (21–10), followed by Cuellar, who went 18–12. Dobson and McNally posted double-digit wins but had losing seasons, with records of 16–18 and 13–17 respectively. Alexander, who came over in the Frank Robinson trade, went 6–8 in nine starts and a total of 35 appearances.

There would be three new faces in the lineup on a regular basis during the 1972 season—outfielder Don Baylor, infielder Bobby Grich, and a future manager of the Orioles, catcher Johnny Oates. Baylor had been named The Sporting News Minor League Player of the Year in 1970 while playing for the Class AAA team in Rochester. He made the season roster in 1972, playing 102 games with 11 home runs and 38 RBIs, while playing behind the starting outfield of Rettenmund, Blair, and Buford. Grich was the 1971 winner of The Sporting News Minor League Player of the Year award for Rochester, and hit .278 with 12 home runs in 1972 while playing both shortstop and second base, appearing in the All-Star Game as a rookie.

Oates shared the catching duties with Etchebarren and posted the best fielding percentage among catchers in the American League. Oates was behind the plate for 82 games. But manager Earl Weaver was always looking for power hitters, and after the season he sent Oates, Dobson, and Davey Johnson (who would eventually become manager of the Orioles a year after Oates was fired) to Atlanta for Earl Williams. Years later, when Oates became a successful major league manager, he credited Weaver as one of the managers he played for and learned from, but it wasn't because of a lot of lengthy discussions about baseball strategy. "When I played for the Orioles, Earl Weaver only spoke to me twice," Oates said. "Once, our catcher got hurt and I said, 'I'll get in there for you, Earl.' He said, 'Fat chance.' After I got traded, he said, 'Enjoy Atlanta.'" Oates passed away from a brain tumor in December 2004.

The 1972 season would be the start of the Oakland A's era of dominance. After losing to the Orioles in the 1971 ALCS, they would defeat the Tigers in five games and go on to beat the Cincinnati Reds in seven games to win the World Series.

The Orioles said good-bye to Buford on February 1, 1973, selling his contract to the Fukuoka Lions in Japan, and picked up the slack with two outstanding rookie outfielders, Al Bumbry and Rich Coggins. Bumbry would bat .337 with 73 runs scored in 110 games to win AL Rookie of the Year honors, while Coggins hit .319 with 41 RBIs in 110 games to finish second in the rookie award voting. The 1973 squad would continue to change the Orioles from a power-hitting team with starters who played nearly every game into more of a line-drive, timely hitting team with platoon players. Williams, the newcomer, would lead the 1973 squad with 22 home runs. After him it was Grich with 12, and Powell and Baylor with 11 each. The

TRIVIA

What did Dave McNally do in 1970 that no other pitcher had ever done?

Answers to the trivia questions are on pages 165–166.

first designated hitter for Baltimore would be former Dodgers out-fielder Tommy Davis, who batted .306 and drove in 89 runs.

This new version of the Orioles would fare much better, coming back to win the AL East title with a record of 97–65, eight games ahead of second-place Boston. Palmer would win 20 games for the fourth straight season, and he captured the AL Cy Young Award with a record of 22–9 and a 2.40 ERA. He came close to both a perfect game and no-hit bids during the season. On June 16 against the Texas Rangers, Palmer retired the first 25 batters before Ken Suarez singled with one out in the ninth inning. Palmer held on for a two-hit 9–1 victory. Then, in the first game of a doubleheader on July 27 against the Cleveland Indians, George Hendrick hit a single in the eighth inning to break up Palmer's no-hit effort.

Palmer would continue his excellence in the AL Championship Series, as Baltimore went up against the defending World Champion Oakland Athletics. On October 6 in Baltimore before a crowd of 41,279 at Memorial Stadium, Palmer struck out 12 in a 6–0 shutout. Meanwhile, over in the National League, it looked as if a rematch of the 1969 World Series was in the making. The Mets turned in another miracle season, winning the NL East with a record barely above .500, going 82–79, and were preparing to face the Reds in the NLCS.

The Orioles, though, couldn't hold up their end. Oakland came back to win Game 2, 6–3, before the disappointed hometown crowd of 48,425 on October 7 behind Catfish Hunter and closer Rollie Fingers. Oakland had home runs by shortstop Bert Campaneris and additional hits by third baseman Sal Bando, who hit two, and out-fielder Joe Rudi. Game 3 on October 9 in Oakland would be the backbreaker—and heartbreaker—for the Orioles, with Cuellar and Ken Holtzman engaged in a pitching duel for the ages. The Orioles took a 1–0 lead in the second inning on a home run by Williams, but the A's came back to tie the score in the bottom of the eighth. A's won it 2–1 in the bottom of the eleventh when Campaneris led off with a home run before a crowd of 34,367.

The next day, in Game 4, Baltimore came back after a 4–0 deficit to tie the game in the seventh inning off Oakland starter Vida Blue, the key hit being Etchebarren's three-run home run. One inning later

27—The number of home runs hit by Reggie
Jackson in an Orioles uniform, leading the club in 1976.

Bobby Grich hit a home run to break the 4–4 tie and give the Orioles a 5–4 win to tie up the series and set up the fifth and deciding game—the first Game 5 Baltimore would play in the ALCS. It turned out to be no contest as Hunter pitched a five-hit 3–0 shutout. The A's would go on to defeat the Mets in seven games to win their second straight World Series championship.

Weaver continued to use his entire roster to platoon players and create matchups at the plate that suited his numbers. And Cashen strengthened an aging pitching staff by trading Rettenmund and infielder Junior Kennedy to the Reds for starting pitcher Ross Grimsley.

The 1974 season opened with Hank Aaron making baseball history on April 8 by passing Baltimore's most famous native son, Babe Ruth, on the all-time home run list, hitting his 715th career shot off Dodgers pitcher Al Downing. Weaver began using a young, talented third baseman named Enos Cabell (who would later go on to be a productive third baseman for the Houston Astros), in a variety of positions—first base, second base, third base, outfield—along with youngsters Bumbry and Coggins. Grich led the team in home runs that year with 19, and as a team they hit 116 home runs. Remarkably, they managed to win the AL East for the second straight year and for the fifth time in six years—again with great pitching and timely hitting, despite the fact that their Cy Young Award winner from the previous year, Palmer, was struggling with elbow problems and they only had a 7–12 record. Cuellar turned in a sterling 22–10 record with a 3.11 ERA, and Grimsley picked up the slack from Palmer, going 18–13. McNally also had a strong season, going 16–10.

In September, Baltimore starters turned in a record-setting series of pitching outings. On September 2, Grimsley and Cuellar each threw 1–0 shutouts against the Red Sox. Two days later, Palmer pitched a 6–0 shutout against Boston. Then, on September 6, McNally and Cuellar each threw shutouts in a doubleheader against the Cleveland Indians,

2–0 and 1–0—the Orioles' fourth and fifth consecutive shutouts and a league record, with 54 straight scoreless innings pitched.

The Orioles would win the AL East with a 91–71 record, finishing ahead of an improved Yankees team by two games, and would face the A's yet again in the ALCS. The Orioles won Game 1 on October 5 before a crowd of 41,609 in Oakland by the score of 6–3, with Cuellar getting the win, backed by home runs from Brooks Robinson, Blair, and Grich. It would be the only game Baltimore would win. In fact, the Orioles offense would score just one run in the rest of the series. Oakland won Game 2 on October 6 before a crowd of 42,810 in on a 5–0 shutout by Holtzman. Back in Baltimore for Game 3, a crowd of 32,060—small by playoff standards—watched Blue out-duel Palmer 1–0; and then an even smaller—embarrassingly small—crowd of 28,136 saw Hunter beat Cuellar 2–1 to clinch the series. Cuellar walked Gene Tenace in the fifth inning to force in a run, and Reggie Jackson doubled in the winning run in the seventh inning. The A's would go on to win their third straight World Series championship, beating the Los Angeles Dodgers in five games.

The poor attendance at the last playoff game in Baltimore would come back to haunt Orioles fans, who had come to expect post-season play as a way of life. That way of life would disappear for the next five years.

Cashen would make two major off-season deals that would dramatically change the franchise. One was trading Cabell and Rob Andrews to the Houston Astros for first baseman Lee May and Jay Schlueter. May would provide the Orioles with a huge power boost and be an influential presence to a rookie who would later become one of the franchise icons. Then Cashen made a bold move, trading away one of the mainstays and fan favorites, McNally, along with Coggins, to the Montreal Expos for outfielder Ken Singleton and pitcher Mike Torrez. Singleton would become one of the stalwarts of the Orioles lineup, as an outfielder and designated hitter, for the next 10 seasons.

He would also make one more deal before the start of the 1975 season that would mark the changing of the guard for the Orioles. Boog Powell was dealt to the Cleveland Indians, along with pitcher Don Hood, for catcher Dave Duncan.

An intimidating force in the middle of the Orioles lineup in the '60s and '70s, first baseman Boog Powell hit 303 home runs in a Baltimore uniform.

Ironically, Powell would be reunited with an old Orioles team-mate in Cleveland, but he would be playing for him instead of playing with him. Frank Robinson made an impact wherever he went, and he would perhaps make his biggest impact on April 8, 1975, when he made his debut as the first black manager in the history of Major League Baseball. As a player-manager, writing himself in the lineup as the designated hitter, Frank Robinson made a dramatic debut by hitting a home run in his first at-bat in a 5–3 win over the Yankees. It was Frank Robinson's eighth Opening Day home run, setting a major league record. He got plenty of help from Powell, who went 3-for-3 with a home run and a double.

The Orioles would compete in 1975 with a 90–69 record, but finish in second place in the division, four-and-a-half games behind the Red Sox. The Red Sox would go on to play the Reds in what was

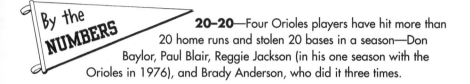

20–20—Four Orioles players have hit more than 20 home runs and stolen 20 bases in a season—Don Baylor, Paul Blair, Reggie Jackson (in his one season with the Orioles in 1976), and Brady Anderson, who did it three times.

considered by many to be one of the greatest World Series ever played—including the dramatic setting for the legendary Game 6 and Carlton Fisk's home run at Fenway Park. May and Baylor would be the big bats for Baltimore, as May hit 20 home runs and drove in 99 runs, while Baylor blasted 25 home runs and drove in 76 runs. Palmer came back to win his second AL Cy Young Award, with a 23–11 record, 10 shutouts, and a 2.09 ERA. Brooks Robinson was very near the end of his career, and managed to hit just six home runs and drive in 53 runs in 144 games. But he was still good enough with the glove to win his last Gold Glove award, the 16th time he received that honor.

McNally would make baseball history off the field. On December 23, 1975, arbitrator Peter Seitz announced a landmark decision that created free agency and declared McNally and Dodgers pitcher Andy Messersmith free agents. But McNally, who had retired on June 8 after going 3–6 in 12 starts for Montreal, remained retired and did not take advantage of the ruling.

Baltimore would compete but fall short again in 1976, finishing second: 10½ games behind the Yankees with a record of 88–74. There would be a changing of the guard in the Orioles front office, as Hank Peters took over as general manager in 1976.

What made this season particularly interesting and unusual for the Orioles was a deal they made just before the start of the season. In an exchange for future free agents once the 1976 season concluded, the Orioles obtained outfielder Reggie Jackson and pitcher Ken Holtzman from Oakland in exchange for pitchers Mike Torrez and Paul Mitchell and outfielder Don Baylor. Jackson would lead the team in home runs with 27, and finish second with 91 RBIs, behind May's 109 runs driven in. Brooks Robinson, at the age of 39, would play in just 71 games and hit only .211, as Weaver began playing his supposed heir apparent, Doug DeCinces, who played in 129 games (109 of them at third base), hitting 11 home runs, driving in 42 runs, and batting .234. Again, pitching carried the day for Baltimore. Palmer won his third Cy Young Award with a record of 22–13 and a 2.51 ERA, beating out rookie sensation Mark "the Bird" Fidrych. Cuellar was done, with a 4–13 record.

The Jackson-Holtzman trade was big news, but it did not have a significant impact on the future of the franchise. The deal they made on June 15, though, would be one of the most important trades in the history of the club. Baltimore dealt pitchers Holtzman, Doyle Alexander, Grant Jackson, and catcher Elrod Hendricks to the Yankees for pitchers Tippy Martinez, Scott McGregor, Rudy May, and Dave Pagan, and catcher Rick Dempsey. McGregor, Dempsey, and Tippy Martinez would become part of the Orioles foundation for the next decade.

In November 1976, free agency began in full force, with Bobby Grich leaving Baltimore and joining Jackson, Baylor, Torrez, Don Gullett, Joe Rudi, Gene Tenace, and Rollie Fingers, among others, as they signed with other teams. It was the beginning of a new era in baseball, and a new era in Orioles history as well.

Earl Weaver

"On my tombstone just write: 'The sorest loser that ever lived.'"

That, in a nutshell, is the philosophy of the legendary Baltimore Orioles manager Earl Weaver, who led his team to four American League pennants and one World Series championship during 17 seasons in Baltimore.

Weaver displayed that soreness over losing so many times on the field that it became a baseball sideshow, something that fans often looked forward to when there was a call by an umpire that did not go the Orioles' way.

He was thrown out of nearly 100 games, including once in 1985 when he was kicked out of both games of a doubleheader. He was tossed out of Game 4 of the 1969 World Series. And his fiery style often clashed with his players, particularly his well-publicized battles with outspoken pitching ace Jim Palmer.

Along the way, though, he won a lot of games—1,480—and his .583 winning percentage ranks fifth on the all-time list of those who managed 10 or more seasons exclusively in the 20th century.

The Orioles had a successful manager in Hank Bauer in 1968. He had led the club to their 1966 World Series championship and three winning seasons in the four he had managed in Baltimore, with a record of 364–281. But his team suffered a losing record of 76–85 in 1967, and after getting off to a slow start in the first half of the 1968 season, falling 10½ games behind the Detroit Tigers, general manager Harry Dalton fired Bauer and replaced him with Weaver, a 37-year-old unknown minor league manager who had been groomed for the job.

Weaver never played in the major leagues, spending time as a second baseman in the Cardinals and Pirates organizations from

1948 through 1957. He stopped playing and began managing in 1956 in Knoxville for the Cardinals organization, then came to the Orioles farm system the following year, and continued at various stops in the system until he got the call to come to Baltimore in 1968. His teams won titles in three different leagues and also finished second five times. He had the touch. Dalton described Weaver as "a winner," and Weaver told writers that he would "rather lose making a move" than by doing nothing.

He immediately had an impact on the club, as they finished strong with a record of 48–34, in second place behind the soon-to-be World Champion Tigers in the last season that baseball's postseason would consist only of the World Series. The powerful Orioles lineup, with such sluggers as Frank Robinson and Boog Powell, was perfectly suited to Weaver's style of managing—going for the three-run home run and a big inning, and using strong pitching to hold those leads.

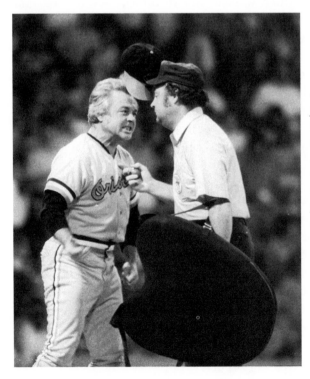

Earl Weaver, protesting a call to umpire Marty Springstead in a 1974 game against the White Sox, had a .583 winning percentage in 18 seasons as the Orioles' manager.

In his first full year in 1969, the leagues were divided up into two divisions, with the Orioles in the American League East. Ultimately, though, it didn't matter how the teams were divided up. Weaver's team was so dominant that it won 109 games, swept the AL West champion Minnesota Twins in three straight in the League Championship Series, and were the favorites to do the same to the improbable National League champions—the Miracle New York Mets.

But the Mets were a team of destiny that year, and they got big home runs and strong pitching from a young standout staff that included Tom Seaver, Jerry Koosman, Gary Gentry, and a young fireballer named Nolan Ryan. They shocked the world and certainly the Orioles and their fans by taking four out of five to win the Series.

It was one of those home runs that set Weaver off in Game 4. Donn Clendenon hit a blast off Orioles starter Mike Cuellar in the second inning at Shea Stadium in New York. Weaver had been voicing his displeasure with the strike zone by home-plate umpire Shag Crawford, who then walked over to the Orioles' dugout and pointed a finger at Weaver, who exploded and came out of the dugout toward Crawford, who then threw Weaver out of the game— the first ejection of a manager in the World Series since 1935.

Weaver would drive his team to nearly the same record in 1970, with 108 wins and another three-game sweep of the Twins. This time, though, their opponent, the Cincinnati Reds, had no special karma on their side, but Weaver had third baseman Brooks Robinson, who showed the world why he was so beloved in Baltimore with his slick fielding and clutch-hitting.

Weaver knew how to manage such talent, and got his team back to the World Series for the third straight time in 1971, winning 101 games and again winning the ALCS in three straight, this time against a team that would soon become their nemesis, a team that would replace the Orioles as the league powerhouse—the Oakland Athletics, led by their young slugger Reggie Jackson and pitchers Catfish Hunter and Vida Blue. But he could not bring a second straight World Series championship to Baltimore, as the Orioles lost to the Pittsburgh Pirates and Roberto Clemente in seven games.

Weaver would, in fact, never again win a World Series championship, though his teams were always in the mix. He lost one of the

TOP 10

Orioles' Managing Records

Manager	Record
1. Earl Weaver	1,480–1,060
2. Paul Richards	517–539
3. Hank Bauer	407–318
4. Johnny Oates	291–270
5. Mike Hargrove	275–372
6. Frank Robinson	230–285
7. Joe Altobelli	212–167
8. Davey Johnson	186–138
9. Billy Hitchcock	163–161
10. Ray Miller	157–167

leaders of the team when Frank Robinson was traded after the 1971 season and his team failed to make the playoffs, finishing in third place in the division with an 80–74 record.

They would be back in the postseason picture in 1973 and 1974, with two AL East division titles, but they lost to Oakland in both of those series. Weaver then helped reconstruct a new version of the Orioles, with new pitchers Scott McGregor and Mike Flanagan and a young first baseman named Eddie Murray, and, under new owner Edward Bennett Williams, Weaver brought Baltimore back to the World Series in 1979. They won 102 games and beat the California Angels in four games in the ALCS. But again they came up short against the Pirates in a seven-game Series, losing 4–3—a devastating defeat because Baltimore had led the Series 3–1.

Still, there was a feeling that these new Orioles were at the start of another dynasty-type run of postseason play, similar to the one that Weaver oversaw when he first arrived. Weaver certainly seemed to think so, based on the declaration he made before Game 6 of the 1979 World Series—that he would retire after the 1982 season.

But the breaks didn't go their way. They won 100 games in 1980—the fifth time Weaver's team won 100 or more—but finished

DID YOU KNOW . . . Earl Weaver's teams won three American League pennants, one World Series, and 318 games from 1969 to 1971. But it wasn't until 1973, when his team bounced back from the 80-win 1972 season to win the AL East again with 97 victories, that Weaver won AL Manager of the Year honors.

second to the New York Yankees. In 1981, the divided strike season, they finished second again with a record of 59–46.

And the most heartbreaking may have been the 1982 season, which came down to the final weekend of the year for the division title against the Milwaukee Brewers. The Orioles had won 94 games and were one game behind the Brewers on the final day of the season. The Orioles were playing at Memorial Stadium before a sellout crowd of 51,642 fans who realized they could be seeing Earl Weaver's last game.

What would have been a storybook ending—the Orioles tying the Brewers for a one-game playoff—did not come to pass, as they lost 10–2, bringing a disappointing ending to the Weaver era. But the postgame celebration was a memorable one, as fans stood and applauded Weaver, who came back onto the field in a emotional scene.

But it clearly ate at Weaver to watch his replacement, Joe Altobelli, manage his team in 1983 to a World Series title—a championship that Weaver surely thought was his. Weaver remained close to owner Edward Bennett Williams, and when Williams fired Altobelli halfway through the 1985 season, he brought Weaver back. The second act, though, was not like the first. They went 53–52 for the rest of the 1985 season, and then Weaver suffered through the only losing year in his major league managing career in 1986, when the Orioles went 73–89. "Everything broke down," Weaver said, in assessing the season. "The 0-for-4's, the left on bases, the pitchers allowing all those home runs. It just added up."

Weaver retired for good this time, and, despite the failure in his comeback, he remained a fan favorite and is still regarded as one of the greatest managers of his time. He had won Manager of the Year honors three times, and in 1996 he was elected to the National Baseball Hall of Fame.

A New Era Begins

There would be a number of new faces on the 1977 Baltimore Orioles roster. There would be the ones who came over in the trade with the Yankees the season before—Tippy Martinez, May, Dempsey, and McGregor. And there would be several young prospects who had come up through the Orioles farm system who would not just blossom, but take their place among the most important players ever to wear an Oriole uniform.

First baseman Eddie Murray and pitchers Mike Flanagan and Dennis Martinez had an immediate impact in their first season in Baltimore, and it was this new, homegrown blood that took many people by surprise. Given the loss of players like Reggie Jackson, Bobby Grich, and 20-game-winner Wayne Garland to free agency, the Orioles expected to struggle in 1977. But thanks to that 1976 trade and the prospects coming through, the club was actually better, winning nine games more than the previous season, ending with a record of 97–64. Unfortunately, what would have been a division-winning record most seasons was only good enough for second place in 1977, and even then they tied the Boston Red Sox behind the division-winning Yankees. The Yankees would win the AL East by two-and-a-half games with a record of 100–62, and go on to win their first World Series since 1962, led by a former one-season Baltimore Oriole—Reggie Jackson.

The arrival of the new talent couldn't have been more opportune, marking the change from one era to another—the beginning of the Eddie Murray era coming in the same season as the Brooks Robinson era came to a close. It spanned nearly the entire history of the Orioles franchise, starting with the six games in which he appeared 22 seasons earlier, in 1955, to this final year of his Hall of

Fame career. He would finish with 268 home runs, 1,357 RBIs, and 2,848 hits—all impressive offensive numbers. But it was his glove that made Brooks Robinson a legend—16 Gold Gloves—and it was his warm personality that made him a Baltimore icon. He would appear in just 24 games in 1977, but he gave Baltimore fans one last dramatic moment to remember on April 19, 1977, in a game at Memorial Stadium against the Cleveland Indians. Pinch-hitting for Larry Harlow, Brooks Robinson hit a three-run homer in the bottom of the tenth inning off Dave LaRoche to beat the Indians 6–5. The day before, against former Orioles pitcher Pat Dobson, Murray had hit his first major league home run.

Baltimore fans officially said good-bye to Brooks Robinson as a ballplayer on September 18, when nearly 52,000 fans filled Memorial Stadium for "Thank Brooks Day." He, along with Johnny Unitas, were two of the biggest icons in the history of the city. As Associated Press reporter Gordon Beard wrote, "Brooks never asked anyone to name a candy bar after him. In Baltimore, people named their children after him."

Brooks Robinson took third base with him—literally—when his heir to the hot corner, Doug DeCinces, took the base out of the ground and handed it to him that day to honor him. Unfortunately for DeCinces, the passing of the torch was never fully accepted by Baltimore fans; DeCinces struggled to gain their approval. He had been groomed to take over for Brooks Robinson since he began seeing regular playing time in 1976, playing in 129 games. He played in 150 games in 1977, hitting 19 home runs, driving in 69 runs, and batting .259. Whatever DeCinces did, though, was never quite good enough, as he was never able to shake the memory of the greatest third baseman in the history of the game, whose presence loomed over third base at Memorial Stadium long after Brooks Robinson was done playing.

When the 1977 season was over, Murray had hit 27 home runs, driven in 88 runs, and batted .283 on his way to AL Rookie of the Year honors. It would be the first in a long career of achievements for Murray, who grew up as one of 11 children in Los Angeles in a family that included four brothers who would also play professional baseball.

By the NUMBERS **3**—The number of times Ray Miller was hired as pitching coach for the Orioles: hired by Earl Weaver to replace George Bamberger in 1977, hired again in 1997 to replace Pat Dobson, and hired one more time in 2004 to replace Mark Wiley.

The left-handed Flanagan made a huge impact as well in his first year, posting a 15–10 record and a 3.64 ERA. Flanagan had been a seventh-round draft choice by Baltimore in June 1973. He spent four years in the minor league system, going 35–16, and Weaver, rightly so, felt Flanagan was ready to come north with the major league club in 1977. He became part of a staff led by Palmer, who went 20–11, winning 20 games for the third straight season and the seventh time in his great career; May, who went 18–14; Ross Grimsley, posting a 14–10 mark; and Dennis Martinez, signed as a free agent out of Nicaragua in 1973, who compiled a 14–7 record.

For his work, Weaver was voted AL Manager of the Year, but he would lose two mainstays on his coaching staff after the 1977 season. Billy Hunter left midway through the 1977 season to take another shot at managing for the Texas Rangers. Pitching coach George Bamberger moved up to manage as well, joining former Orioles general manager Harry Dalton in Milwaukee to manage the Brewers after the season.

Those moves resulted in a little bizarre horse-trading to replenish Weaver's staff with coaches the Orioles organization was comfortable with—coaches who knew how the franchise conducted the business of baseball. When Hunter put together his new Rangers coaching staff, he hired a respected minor league pitching coach in the Orioles farm system named Ray Miller. Several days later, when Baltimore lost its pitching coach with Bamberger's departure, Orioles general manager Hank Peters quickly asked for permission from the Rangers to talk to their new pitching coach. Miller came back to the Orioles organization to join Weaver's staff.

To replace Hunter, Weaver called on one of his closest confidants, a baseball lifer whom he had managed more than 25 years ago, and who had gone on to become one of the most influential figures in the Orioles minor league system as a manager in the organization from 1961 to 1974—Cal Ripken Sr. He had been Weaver's bullpen coach since 1976, but moved to the third base box when Hunter left.

His influence would extend far beyond the third base line, and that didn't just consist of raising a future Orioles icon, Cal Jr., and another son, Billy, a major league player who would wear the Orioles uniform. As a minor league manager, he taught generations about the "Oriole Way"—the right way to fundamentally approach the game. "We always talked about the 'Oriole Way,'" Ray Miller said. "Cal Ripken Sr. was the one who indoctrinated every one of us who came in."

General manager Hank Peters made another off-season move to fine tune the team according to Weaver's liking on December 7 by trading three pitchers—May, Randy Miller, and Bryn Smith—to the Montreal Expos for outfielder Gary Roenicke and pitchers Don Stanhouse and Joe Kerrigan. Roenicke would be an integral part of one of the greatest outfield platoons in recent times, along with John Lowenstein. Stanhouse would be the Orioles closer for the next two years, recording 45 saves and causing Weaver's smoking addiction to grow with some of his precarious performances out of the bullpen. Finally closing out a victory, Stanhouse earned the nickname "Fullpack" from his manager.

The Orioles continued to play winning baseball in 1978, winning 90 games or more for the ninth time in the 11 seasons Weaver had managed the team, with a record of 90–71. But they were stuck in the most competitive division in baseball, and that record would net them just a fourth-place finish, nine games behind the division winners, the New York Yankees, who won the title after the Red Sox's historic collapse in the final weeks of the season, blowing their comfortable division lead as the Yankees caught them, resulting in a tie at the end of the regular season and the one-game playoff at Fenway Park where Bucky Dent hit a three-run home run in the seventh inning off former Orioles pitcher Mike Torrez on their way to a 5–4 New York win. The Yankees would defeat the

TRIVIA

How many home runs did Reggie Jackson hit in his one and only season with the Orioles?

Answers to the trivia questions are on pages 165–166.

Cal Ripken Sr. and son Cal Jr. here on Father's Day at Yankee Stadium on June 20, 1982. Cal Sr. managed the Orioles for one full season and parts of two others.

Kansas City Royals in four games in the ACLS and win their second consecutive World Series championship in six games against the Los Angeles Dodgers.

Baltimore's offense produced the most power it had in recent years. DeCinces had his best season as an Oriole, leading the team with 28 home runs and bringing home 80 runs. Murray hit 27 home runs for the second straight season and led the team with 95 RBIs. Designated hitter Lee May slugged 25 home runs and had 80 RBIs. Singleton hit 20 home runs, drove in 81 runs, and led the team in batting with a .293 average.

But their increased power—154 home runs—did not translate to more runs scored, as they lost their leadoff batter, Al Bumbry. On May 12, in a 9–3 loss to the Rangers, Bumbry broke his leg sliding into second base. He would return in September for a handful of pinch-hitting appearances. The year before, in 133 games, Bumbry batted 317 and scored 74 runs, ranking fourth on a team that had scored 719 runs total. In 1978, the Orioles would score 659 runs.

Like clockwork, Palmer won 20 games for the fourth straight year and the eighth time in his career, going 21–12 with a 2.46 ERA—just the sixth pitcher in the 20th century to have accomplished that feat.

TRIVIA

What famous NBA player was Orioles pitcher Mike Flanagan's basketball teammate at the University of Massachusetts?

Answers to the trivia questions are on pages 165–166.

Over a nine-year period, Palmer had a record of 176–97 with a 2.54 ERA. Flanagan nearly won 20 games as well, with a 19–15 record, and came close to getting a no-hitter in the last week of the season. On September 26, Flanagan had no-hit the Cleveland Indians through eight-and-two-thirds innings when, needing just one out, he gave up a home run to Gary Alexander. Flanagan gave up two more singles, and Stanhouse came in to save the 3–1 victory.

Dennis Martinez followed Flanagan (going 16–11) and Scott McGregor, who emerged as a quality starter with a 15–13 record and a 3.32 ERA in 32 starts. And in his one pitching outing that year, catcher Elrod Hendricks—who returned to the Orioles after the 1977 trade to New York as a free agent for the 1978 season—allowed one hit and walked one batter in two-and-one-third innings pitched, in one of the more bizarre games in franchise history.

On June 26 against the Toronto Blue Jays the Orioles were losing 19–6 in just the fifth inning and Weaver did not want to waste any more pitchers. So he sent outfielder Larry Harlow to the mound to pitch. Harlow retired two batters, walked three, threw a wild pitch, then gave up a single, another walk, and a three-run home run by John Mayberry. Toronto now led 24–6, so Weaver called on Hendricks, who shut out the Blue Jays for two-and-one-half innings. Stanhouse took over in the eighth inning of the game, which ended with Toronto winning 24–10.

Hendricks did not have any pitching outings in 1979, as the Orioles staff, carried by the left arm of Flanagan, did not have the need for much duty from position players. The hurlers took care of their own business that season.

Coming Up Short

A deep pitching staff got even deeper when the Orioles signed free agent pitcher Steve Stone in November 1978. And they strengthened their bench—and gave Weaver one of the greatest outfield platoons in recent memory—when in the same month, they picked up utility outfielder John Lowenstein. Both would be key contributors to what would be the year the Orioles would return to a once-familiar place—postseason play.

It didn't start out that way, as Baltimore lost eight of its first 11 games, though one of those wins, a 5–3 Opening Day victory on April 5 against the Chicago White Sox, was Weaver's 1,000th major league managerial victory. But after Palmer beat the Yankees 6–3 on April 19, the Orioles went on a nine-game winning streak. They reached first place on May 18 and, with the exception of one day, led the division for the rest of the 1979 season—a year of "Oriole Magic" at Memorial Stadium.

Murray supplied a lot of that magic with his bat. On May 8, Murray, May, and Roenicke hit consecutive home runs in the sixth inning of an 8–2 win over Oakland, as Murray extended his hit streak to 19 games.

On June 22, DeCinces hit a dramatic two-run home run in the bottom of the ninth for a 6–5 victory over the Detroit Tigers, and the day after that pinch-hitter Terry Crowley delivered the game-winning hit with an RBI single for another 6–5 win.

Though there were many contributors to the magic that season, the one who contributed the most offensively was Singleton, who had a career year, hitting 35 home runs, driving in 111 runs, and batting .295, finishing second in the league MVP voting. And the man with the magic on the mound was Flanagan, who posted a 23–9 mark to capture the AL Cy Young Award. He was one of six Orioles pitchers who registered double-digit wins that year on their way to a 102–57 record, finishing eight games ahead of the Brewers, managed by the former Baltimore pitching coach, George Bamberger.

But perhaps the single biggest reason the Orioles won the division in 1979 was the return of Bumbry, who came back to play 148 games, score 80 runs, steal 37 bases, and bat .285.

Baltimore baseball fans certainly caught on to the magic. The club drew nearly 1.7 million, a franchise record and more than 600,000 ahead of the previous season, and Memorial Stadium was sold out for

The final out of the 1979 World Series, which the Pirates won in seven games. The Orioles won 102 games that year and, despite falling just short of a championship, captivated the Baltimore fans like never before.

Game 1 of the ALCS against the California Angels, with a crowd of 52,787 on hand to watch a matchup of legends—Palmer vs. Nolan Ryan. They saw a classic on October 3, tied at 3–3 going into the bottom of the tenth inning when Weaver sent Lowenstein

TRIVIA

What league award did Ken Singleton win in 1982?

Answers to the trivia questions are on pages 165–166.

up to pinch-hit with two men on base, and he blasted a game-winning three-run home run for a 6–3 victory. It was the first pinch-hit home run in the history of League Championship Series play.

The next day, the Orioles appeared to have it won after three innings, scoring nine runs, led by a three-run Murray home run, to take a 9–1 lead with Flanagan on the mound. But the Angels scored four runs off Flanagan in the seventh and eighth innings, and then Stanhouse gave Weaver a nicotine fit by surrendering two more runs before finally closing out a 9–8 Baltimore victory. When the series moved back to Anaheim on October 5, the Orioles seemed on the verge of a sweep as they led 3–2 going into the bottom of the ninth. But the Angels scored two runs off Dennis Martinez and Stanhouse for a 4–3 win before a crowd of 43,199. But McGregor clinched it by shutting out California in Game 4 by a score of 8–0, with the big hit a three-run home run by designated hitter Pat Kelly.

The Orioles would return to the World Series for the first time since 1971, and ironically they would be facing an old nemesis, the team that had beaten them in seven games in that 1971 Series—the Pittsburgh Pirates. The Pirates battled the Montreal Expos for the NL East until the final game of the season, winning the division with a record of 98–64. They swept the Reds in three straight in the NLCS, and traveled to Baltimore to face the Orioles in Game 1.

The Pirates—a team that had come together during the season, identifying with the pop song by the group Sister Sledge called "We Are Family"—were led by one of the players they had faced back in 1971, first baseman Willie "Pops" Stargell, who was co-MVP in the NL with Keith Hernandez. Stargell had 32 home runs and drove in 82 runs, and he was joined by All-Star outfielder Dave Parker, who hit 25 home runs, led the team with 94 RBIs, and batted .310; Bill Madlock, who batted .328; and center fielder Omar Moreno, who led the league with 77 stolen bases. Like the Orioles, the Pirates had six pitchers with victories in the double digits, but none who had been as dominant as Flanagan or who had the Hall of Fame credential that Palmer did. Pittsburgh's best starter was John Candelaria, who had a 14–9 record and a 3.22 ERA.

The Orioles went into the Series as the favorite. Former Yankees manager Bob Lemon, who had been fired during the season, wrote a pre-Series analysis for *The New York Times* that claimed Baltimore was a club that didn't "have any weaknesses, as far as I can see. They score runs, and they don't allow very many."

Game 1 was rained out, so they played the next day on October 10 before a crowd of 53,735 at Memorial Stadium, and, with Flanagan facing Bruce Kison, the Orioles appeared to be coasting to a win, as they scored five runs in the bottom of the first inning. But the Pirates fought back, scoring four to make it close, before Flanagan managed to hold Pittsburgh off for a 5–4 complete-game win. The Pirates beat Stanhouse in Game 2 by the score of 3–2, when, with the score tied at 2–2 in the top of the ninth, Manny Sanguillen— who had also been part of that 1971 World Championship squad that had beaten the Orioles—had the game-winning pinch-hit single. Going to Pittsburgh, momentum seemed to be in favor of the Pirates. But the Orioles stunned the nearly 51,000 fans who came to Three Rivers Stadium for Games 3 and 4 on October 12 and 13. The Orioles won 8–4 and 9–6, behind McGregor and Tim Stoddard in relief. Stoddard even got an RBI single, his first professional hit, in the Game 4 victory. Pittsburgh managed to hold off elimination in Game 5 by rocking Flanagan and posting a 7–1 win with Bert Blyleven on the mound, getting the win in relief of starter Jim Rooker. Going back to Baltimore leading three games to two, the Orioles appeared to be a lock to win the Series.

But the only thing that locked up were the Orioles hitters, who scored just one run in the final two games, as the Pirates won the Series—a 4–0 combined shutout by Candelaria and Kent Tekulve against Palmer in Game 6 and a 4–1 victory in Game 7 over McGregor, with reliever Grant Jackson getting the victory. The Orioles were stunned by the defeat, because they felt they had missed the opportunities they had to win. "We knew we had blown

Twenty-three times Orioles pitchers have won 20 games. Jim Palmer won 20 eight times, Dave McNally four, and Mike Cuellar three times. Steve Stone has the club record for most wins in a season, with 25 in 1980, when the Orioles set a record with at least one 20-game winner from 1968 to 1980.

that Series," Rick Dempsey said looking back. "A lot of things went against us in those three games. We hit some balls really good, but the Pirates turned double plays on balls that should have been base hits. We didn't get any breaks, and they got the momentum. They were a high-intensity ballclub, and we just couldn't get anything going."

It would have been a meaningful World Series championship for the Orioles because the owner who had overseen this stretch of excellence was selling the club. Jerry Hoffberger sold the Orioles to someone who would be a very different owner than the brewery magnate. Then again, there weren't too many people anywhere who were quite like Edward Bennett Williams.

The Washington trial lawyer was one of the most powerful men in the most powerful city in the world. He represented such clients as mafia boss Frank Costello, Senator Joe McCarthy, and Teamsters Union President Jimmy Hoffa. He was also the lawyer for *The Washington Post,* and would later press the battle for the paper to publish the Pentagon Papers, going to war with the Nixon White House. He became wealthy as a lawyer, charging a reported $1,000 an hour, and his wealth allowed him to buy into sports franchises such as the Washington Redskins, and now the Orioles, for a sales price of $12.5 million. Williams was a larger-than-life figure, and he had different plans as owner than Hoffberger had. One was not to simply sit back and let the baseball people run the show. He was too opinionated and impatient for that. The other difference was to make a concerted effort, with the absence of baseball in Washington, to market the Orioles as a regional franchise—Washington's team as well as Baltimore's. Many fans suspected that Williams would eventually try to move the franchise to Washington.

Remarkably, the Orioles had nearly as good a season in 1980 as they did in 1979, winning 100 games. Murray had his best season yet, slugging 32 home runs, driving in 116 runs, and batting .300. So did Bumbry, who hit .318, scored 118 runs, had 205 hits (with 29 doubles, 9 triples, and 9 home runs), and 44 stolen bases. The pitching staff was brilliant again, as Stone had a career year, winning the AL Cy Young Award with a 25–7 record, followed by a 20–8 record by McGregor. Palmer and Flanagan won 16 games each. Under the direction of Williams and his close associate, attorney Larry Lucchino, the Orioles' marketing effort managed to draw even more people than the 1979 pennant-winning season, as nearly 1.8 million came to Memorial Stadium. But all that was only good for second place in the division, as the Yankees, under manager Dick Howser, won 103 games.

Nothing went right in baseball in 1981, when a players' strike shut down the game for seven weeks, starting in mid-June. That resulted in two separate seasons, and the Orioles frustratingly finished second in both of them, finishing with an overall record of 59–46. Their pitching suffered when Steve Stone, struggling with elbow tendinitis, had a dismal record of 4–7 and retired at the end of the season.

The only noteworthy event for the franchise that year was the appearance of a tall, rangy 21-year-old hometown boy from Aberdeen, Maryland, who appeared in 23 games in the final month of the season. He had very familiar last name to Orioles fans—Ripken, as in Cal, the son of the Orioles coach. Playing third base, he had just five hits in 39 at-bats, but Weaver saw a player destined for greatness, and knew that Cal Jr. would not be going back to the minor leagues. That was apparent when, on January 28, 1982, the Orioles traded their third baseman, DeCinces, to the Angels for outfielder Dan Ford.

There was a lot of anticipation heading into the 1982 season, because it was to be Weaver's last as an Orioles manager. During the 1979 World Series, Weaver had announced he would stop managing after 1982, and he had stuck by that commitment. He may have expected to win a few World Series by the time 1982 rolled around, given the team he had and where they were when he made the announcement—on the brink of winning the World Series title, although they would lose to the Pirates. So this was a season where part of the rallying cry was to win it for Earl.

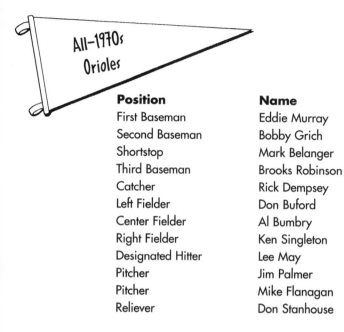

Position	Name
First Baseman	Eddie Murray
Second Baseman	Bobby Grich
Shortstop	Mark Belanger
Third Baseman	Brooks Robinson
Catcher	Rick Dempsey
Left Fielder	Don Buford
Center Fielder	Al Bumbry
Right Fielder	Ken Singleton
Designated Hitter	Lee May
Pitcher	Jim Palmer
Pitcher	Mike Flanagan
Reliever	Don Stanhouse

The problem was, no one told the Milwaukee Brewers about those plans. The Brewers, under former Orioles general manager Harry Dalton, had become the same sort of model player-development organization that Dalton had helped build in Baltimore, with such star players as Robin Yount, Cecil Cooper, and Paul Molitor. They had finished just behind the Orioles in third place in the AL East in 1980 with a record of 86–76, and had passed Baltimore in 1981, with a 62–47 record in the strike-shortened season. The Brewers had struggled early in the year, but after firing manager Buck Rodgers and putting batting coach Harvey Kuenn in the job, Milwaukee went on a 72–43 run in the last two-thirds of the season.

Even though they had built up a seven-and-a-half game lead over the Orioles by mid-August, Baltimore got even hotter, winning 30 of their last 40 games before a final weekend showdown against the Brewers at Memorial Stadium. Four games behind Milwaukee, the Orioles swept a doubleheader, 8–3 and 7–1, then followed that up with an 11–3 win on Saturday. The Orioles were one game behind the Brewers on the final day of the season, playing at home, with Palmer on the mound facing Don Sutton. It seemed to all line up for Baltimore. "In that last game, we had our ace going, Palmer, and I thought we were going to win it," Tippy Martinez said. But they came up short, losing 10–2, with two home runs by Yount and a rally-ending catch by left-fielder Ben Oglivie in the eighth inning, when Baltimore was down just 5–2.

The Orioles finished with a 94–68 record in Weaver's good-bye year. Murray led the team with 32 home runs, 110 RBIs, and a .316 average. Ripken proved Weaver right by hitting 28 home runs and driving in 93 runs to win the AL Rookie of the Year award. He also proved Weaver right about where he should play. Weaver was convinced Ripken could play shortstop in the major leagues, and Ripken played more there—94 games—than he had at third base that season. Dennis Martinez led the rotation with a 16–12 record, followed by Flanagan at 15–11, and Palmer, who had a remarkable year, posting a 15–5 mark. It would be the last great hurrah for the hurler.

Despite the loss, the sellout crowd of 51,642 fans stayed long after the game to pay tribute to a tearful Weaver, who came back on the field, followed by many of his players, for an emotional sendoff. "That was a sad day, and it was doubly disappointing because it was Earl's last game," Rick Dempsey said.

Williams wanted to hire Frank Robinson to replace Weaver, but he was managing the San Francisco Giants, and they refused to give the Orioles permission to talk to Robinson and did not inform him that Baltimore had asked to talk to him. General manager Hank Peters wanted to hire John McNamara, and Weaver lobbied for Cal Sr. to replace him. Williams and Peters decided on a compromise candidate—former Giants manager Joe Altobelli, who had been running the Orioles Class AAA club in Rochester.

For all intents and purposes, though, it really didn't matter who was managing the team the next season. This was an Orioles squad that still carried the pain of losing the 1979 World Series, and the disappointments that came after that of just falling short. They sensed time was running out, and they knew what they had to do. This team was ready to manage itself.

Trying Times

The 1983 Orioles said hello to a new face—center fielder John Shelby, who would platoon with Al Bumbry that year—and another young pitcher named Storm Davis who emerged from the farm system. But they would say good-bye to a longtime fan favorite, pinch-hitter Terry Crowley, as new manager Joe Altobelli and general manager Hank Peters opted to keep outfielder Jim Dwyer instead for the final roster spot.

There would be another new face on the scene, this one in the broadcast booth. Longtime Orioles announcer and future Hall of Famer Chuck Thompson was leaving radio and switching to television. He was replaced by a relatively unknown 31-year-old announcer from Boston, where he had been the second announcer on Red Sox games—Jon Miller. He would become an announcing legend for the Orioles.

The Orioles had become more popular under Williams's ownership than ever before, despite not reaching the playoffs since 1979. They drew 1.6 million in 1982, the third highest total in franchise history. Baltimore was undergoing a transformation from a football town to a baseball city, as the Baltimore Colts, under controversial owner Bob Irsay, had fallen on hard times and angered much of their fan base in Baltimore. In 1984, Baltimore would become a baseball town by default, as the unimaginable happened—the Colts left town and moved to Indianapolis.

So when the 1983 season opened, all of the focus was on the Orioles and how they would fare without Earl Weaver. Altobelli got off to a rocky start, as his team lost 7–2 to the Kansas City Royals before a sold-out crowd of 51,889 fans at Memorial Stadium. Cal Ripken committed an error, and Dan Ford—whose poor performance in 1982 had made him the target of the wrath of Orioles fans (after coming over in the trade that sent Doug DeCinces to the Angels)—failed to catch a pop-up in the first inning. Dennis Martinez was the losing pitcher—a sign of things to come for the Orioles starter that season. Jim Palmer, the scheduled Opening Day pitcher, had to be scratched because of lower-back problems—a sign of things to come for the future Hall of Fame pitcher who was on the last leg of a brilliant career.

Dennis Martinez was a talented but troubled ballplayer whose alcohol problems would become public at the end of that year, when he was arrested and jailed for drunken driving in Baltimore in December. His career hit rock bottom in 1983. He fell out of favor with Altobelli and, between starting appearances and banishments to the bullpen, finished with a 7–16 record. When one of your starters falls that far, you'd better have others ready to pick up the slack. Mike Flanagan picked it up, and then some.

The Orioles left-hander would be an anchor for the staff in the early part of the 1983 season, when the team was plagued by inconsistent play. Baltimore was at .500 after the first eight games of the season when Flanagan pitched a complete-game 6–1 win over the Cleveland Indians. Despite a groin pull in his next start, he would help shut out the Athletics in a 6–0 win after that, keeping the club above 500 with a 10–8 record. Mike Flanagan and Scott McGregor, who won his first two starts, were the only two starters that Altobelli could rely on. Then there were Dennis Martinez's woes, and those of Palmer, who, after several starts, was sidelined again with back spasms that would put him on the disabled list. But this was the year the Orioles' farm system would serve them best—for the last time. They had a young pitcher named Storm Davis, who had come up

By the NUMBERS 5—The number of American League Most Valuable Player awards for Orioles players—Brooks Robinson (1964), Frank Robinson (1966), Boog Powell (1970), and Cal Ripken (1983 and 1991).

Dennis Martinez, here against the Angels winning his 100th career game, spent the first 10 years of his long career with the Orioles.

from Class AAA Rochester during the 1982 season and had gone 8–4, to step in from his role as spot starter and long reliever to fill Palmer's role. But then Baltimore needed someone to take the place of Davis, and they called on Rochester to deliver another promising pitching prospect, one who had been stuck with the Red Wings for three straight seasons, held back because of the pitching depth on the major league roster.

By the time Mike Boddicker was sent down to Rochester during spring training of 1983, he had compiled an impressive minor league record of 52–37 with a 3.30 ERA, but was long overdue to get his shot with Baltimore, and was thinking it was never going to happen. "My situation was that I had four Cy Young winners ahead of me in Baltimore," Boddicker said. "I figured if I kept pitching well down in the minors, sooner or later I would become a minor league free agent

That the 1980 Orioles, who won 100 games, were only 28–30 on June 14.

and somebody would want me. I figured I could bide my time as long as I could pitch well."

Finally, Boddicker was getting the call up when it counted (he had been part of the September roster expansion promotions the three previous seasons). But Peters made it clear it would only be temporary. "Don't give up your apartment in Rochester," Peters told Boddicker. "As soon as Palmer is back, you're going down again."

They could afford to plug in a Boddicker for a Palmer at the end of his career, in large part because of the pitching of McGregor and particularly Flanagan, who pitched a 1–0 shutout against the Seattle Mariners to give Baltimore a 17–12 record, and gave the left-hander a 6–0 record for the 1983 season. The club was on a four-game winning streak when they faced the Rangers in one of the more legendary games of that year, one that has made its way into Orioles lore.

Ken Kaiser was the first-base umpire for that game. He was a former professional wrestler and bouncer from Rochester, and it was there a feud began with a young Orioles prospect named Eddie Murray. Those tensions carried over to the major leagues, and came to a head in Texas that day. In the bottom of the first inning, Larry Parrish checked his swing on one pitch from Dennis Martinez, and home-plate umpire Rick Reed called the pitch a ball. Catcher Rick Dempsey appealed the call to Kaiser at first base, and he upheld Reed's call over Dempsey's objections. Kaiser fully expected Murray to argue as well, so he folded his arms and stared at Murray, who in turn folded his arms and stared back. Kaiser screamed at Murray, "You're mimicking me," and ordered Murray to unfold his arms. Murray refused, so Kaiser kicked him out, even though Murray had never said a word to Kaiser. Altobelli came out and argued, and he was thrown out as well, which amused Ken Singleton, as it carried on an Orioles tradition. "When Eddie got ejected, Earl [Weaver] usually did as well," he said. "We called them father and son ejections. Earl felt that we really lost a chance to win when Eddie got kicked out of a game."

The Orioles lost 2–1 and returned home to Memorial Stadium for an important series against the Chicago White Sox, starting with a twi-night doubleheader on May 17. Even though the White Sox were in the AL West, the games against the Orioles that year took on the intensity of division rivals, as if both teams knew they were destined to meet in the postseason. Their unbeatable ace, Flanagan, was starting the first game, with his 6–0 record and having won 13 of his last 14 starts at home, so they liked their chances to win.

They didn't expect their whole season to appear to collapse, though. After Flanagan retired the first batter he faced, Tony Bernazard came up and hit a dribbler between the mound and home plate. Flanagan attempted to come off the mound to field it, but he caught his spikes, twisted his left knee, and had to leave the game. Tim Stoddard came in and pitched five-and-two-thirds innings of relief in a 7–2 Baltimore victory. And there should have been much to feel good about in the second game, as Boddicker, making his debut as a starter, pitched a five-hit 5–0 shutout, putting the Orioles record at 21–13. But the focus was on Flanagan and what turned out to be a serious loss, as the tough left-hander suffered a partial ligament tear that doctors estimated would keep him sidelined for three months.

Oriole Magic

The Baltimore Orioles would be fighting to win the AL East with a new manager and a pitching staff that had lost Mike Flanagan and Jim Palmer and had to suffer with an erratic Dennis Martinez. It wasn't a promising outlook, but the organization that had been the model of excellence since 1966 would take up the slack, and Mike Boddicker would be proof of that, as he finished the season with a 16–8 record and a 2.77 ERA. His teammates had seen enough of him that they were confident he could step up and keep the team in a position to win. Boddicker said his adjustment was easier because of the confidence he had in his teammates. "Everybody contributed on that team," he said. "Everybody knew their role and what they were supposed to do."

Dan Ford had a role in 1983, and it was to convince Orioles fans that he wasn't the player they hated in 1982, when he batted just .235 with 10 home runs and 43 RBIs in 123 games. He won Baltimore fans over in 1983 by getting key hits in big games. In fact, it seemed like nearly every hit Disco Dan had in 1983 was a big hit—like the one he had on May 18, the day after the Orioles swept the White Sox in the doubleheader that saw Flanagan go down. With no score by either team through seven-and-one-third innings, and Chicago starter Richard Dotson throwing a no-hitter, Ford hit a solo home run in the bottom of the eighth inning for a 1–0 Baltimore victory. After the game, while Ford was visiting someone in the Baltimore hotel the White Sox were staying at, he had an amusing encounter with Dotson and his father. "We were in an elevator together," Ford said. "His father said, 'You're Dan Ford, the guy that broke up my son's no-hitter.'" Ford answered, "Yup, I'm the one."

The next night at Exhibition Stadium in Toronto, Ford struck again—this time on his 31st birthday—in the eighth inning again. With the Orioles down 1–0, Ford slammed a two-run, game-winning home run for a 2–1 win. The timely hitting was the perfect complement to the outstanding pitching the Orioles were getting, even with the loss of Flanagan and the erratic Dennis Martinez. McGregor allowed just one run on six hits and no walks in eight-and-one-third innings in that 2–1 win over Toronto. Baltimore had now won eight out of nine games and had a 23–13 record. Then the big hits disappeared, and the hot pitching bubble burst.

The Orioles lost seven in a row, and had fallen to a third-place tie with the Brewers in the AL East, behind the Red Sox and Blue

Orioles fans turned out by the thousands to honor catcher Rick Dempsey and his 1983 teammates for their World Series win over the Phillies.

Jays; although they were still just two games out of first place with a record of 23–20. They managed to stop the losing streak with a 7–4 win over Kansas City behind Storm Davis. They managed to battle back into first place with a 30–23 record, and then called on the farm system once again for pitching help, as Palmer remained sidelined, by bringing up young right-hander Allan Ramirez from Rochester. In his first start against the Milwaukee Brewers, Ramirez did his job by keeping his team in the game after seven innings, with the score tied at 2–2. Home runs by Cal Ripken and John Lowenstein gave the Orioles a 7–3 win. Baltimore swept the series against Milwaukee, with a 33–23 record, taking a three-game lead in the AL East.

TRIVIA

How many more runs did the Orioles score than the Brewers in the first three games of the epic four-game Series to close out the 1982 season?

Answers to the trivia questions are on pages 165–166.

Palmer finally came back, but was being eased into the rotation. He made an appearance as a reliever in a remarkable come-from-behind 11–8 win over the Brewers on June 15, after being down 7–0. Palmer gave up two runs on four hits in three innings of relief. He was scheduled to stay in the bullpen until he felt comfortable returning to the rotation, but Storm Davis got sick, and Dennis Martinez's short stints—he lasted just one-and-two-thirds innings in a 5–3 loss on June 17 against Boston, already his 10th loss of the season—forced Palmer to jump back into the rotation. He had not started since April 26, but he came through and pitched 5⅓ innings of shutout baseball in a 6–3 win over the Red Sox.

Handling Palmer was perhaps Altobelli's biggest challenge. The veteran pitcher was known for his battles with Weaver, but Altobelli did not carry the same weight and could not engage in the same sort of relationship. "I told him that I couldn't do the same thing that Earl did with him," Altobelli said. "I didn't want to fight with him, and when I hear something negative coming out of your mouth, you're coming out of the game. He could pitch four or five innings for you, pitch no-hit ball, and come in and say that his arm is stiff. What happens is you send him out the next inning, and he gets crushed. So he tells the press, 'I told Altobelli that my arm was stiffening up,' and they would all come running to me.'

Despite the volatility of Palmer's status, Boddicker continued to pitch far beyond his rookie years, and McGregor remained nearly unhittable at times. Storm Davis came back from his sickbed to nearly pitch a no-hitter against Detroit. It wasn't until former Michigan quarterback Rick Leach, pinch-hitting in the top of the ninth, slammed a solo home run that the Tigers got a hit. Tippy Martinez would preserve the 3–1 victory for Davis. It was clear as the All-Star break neared that this season would rest on the pitching—even in its fragile, uncertain state. So Hank Peters made a deal to solidify that pitching by shoring up the infield defense, acquiring one of the more colorful characters for the Orioles that year—third baseman Todd Cruz, otherwise known as the "Watchman."

Todd Cruz got the nickname Watchman because, in 1981 after a drinking binge, he broke into a department store and stole dozens of watches. But he fell asleep in the store with his pockets stuffed with watches, and the police found him. But while Cruz was a troubled soul, he was considered a magician with a glove, a former shortstop with a legendary throwing arm. Leo Hernandez, with 13 errors and a lack of range, wasn't getting it done for the Orioles, so they got Cruz, warts and all, from the Seattle Mariners, to fix that hole.

Fix it he did. Cruz gave the Orioles the defense they needed to back up their pitching. "The biggest move we made was when we got Todd Cruz from Seattle," Joe Altobelli said.

They would need all the defense they could muster because the pitching remained unsettled. Palmer went on the disabled list for a second time because of triceps tendinitis. The Orioles, though, were hanging tough at 42–34, in second place in the AL East, just one game out of first at the All-Star break. Cal Ripken and Eddie Murray were both named to the AL squad, though neither one had been elected as a starter. But the focus for the Orioles during the All-Star break was on one of their reliable but eccentric relievers, Sammy Stewart, who was arrested and charged with driving while intoxicated on the Baltimore Beltway. They were also dealing with a mysterious ailment that had hit Tippy Martinez, which turned out to be appendicitis. Tippy Martinez was the anchor of the bullpen,

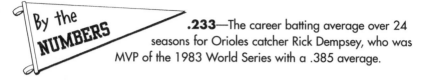

having made 34 appearances with 10 saves and a 5–3 record. But temporarily losing Martinez turned out to be the saving grace of the season for Baltimore.

They would desperately need Martinez during their remarkable pennant stretch run of the 1983 season, and the time off recovering from appendicitis would save his arm from what would have certainly been overuse. "It was a blessing in disguise," said bullpen coach Elrod Hendricks. "When he came back, he picked up right where he left off."

Tippy Martinez was a big part of the 1983 championship run, as were Mike Boddicker, Eddie Murray, Cal Ripken, and others. But there were plenty of small parts who played a big role at key moments. One of them was Bill Swaggerty, a last-minute call-up from Class AAA Rochester to face the AL West's powerful Chicago White Sox on August 13. The Orioles rotation was hurt and worn and had lost seven in a row. On this Saturday in Chicago, they needed something to turn things around.

Swaggerty did, holding the mighty White Sox lineup to two runs after six innings, leaving the game with the scored tied at 2–2. Sammy Stewart and Tippy Martinez pitched shutout relief for three innings, and Ripken broke the game open with a two-run home run in the eighth inning for a 5–2 Baltimore win. Swaggerty didn't get the win, and was sent back down to Rochester after Jim Palmer came off the disabled list, but his impact was huge. Not only did his start put an end to the Orioles' losing streak, but they went 34–10 in their final 44 games after Swaggerty's appearance to run away with the AL East.

They would face the White Sox, the AL West champions, in the League Championship Series. Chicago was a team with quality hitters like Harold Baines and Ron Kittle, and tremendous starting pitching—La Marr Hoyt, the Cy Young Award winner who went 24–10 that year; Richard Dotson, another 20-game winner (22–7); Floyd Bannister; Britt Burns; and former New York Met left-hander Jerry Koosman as the fifth starter.

There was bad blood between the two teams that developed during their regular season games, with brushback pitching and umpire-baiting. With both teams fielding standout pitching, there was little room for error. The Orioles came up short in Game 1 before a home crowd of 51,289, losing 2–1 at Memorial Stadium. Boddicker, their savior, came back to win Game 2, shutting out Chicago 4–0, striking out 14. In that game, Boddicker hit Tom Paciorek and Greg Luzinski with breaking balls, and it did not seem to be intentional. But the White Sox thought it was, and it set the stage for a wild Game 3. Baltimore took an early 4–0 lead, and then Mike Flanagan hit Kittle with a 3–2 pitch. Kittle was held back from rushing the mound, and the benches emptied. Later in the game, Ripken was hit with a pitch, and Murray, the next batter, had a ball sail over his head. Both dugouts ran out of the field, but no punches were thrown. Baltimore did some damage in the game, pummeling Chicago 11–1, and went on to win the five-game ALCS with a 3–0 shutout in Game 4.

TRIVIA

How did reliever Tippy Martinez get three outs in a game against the Toronto Blue Jays without getting any batters out?

Answers to the trivia questions are on pages 165–166.

They would face the Philadelphia Phillies in the World Series, led by veterans Mike Schmidt and Gary Matthews and former Red Machine stars Pete Rose and Joe Morgan.

The Orioles lost the opener at home 2–1, but they were determined not to let this World Series slip away from them like the one against the Pittsburgh Pirates four years earlier. Boddicker won Game 2 4–1, as Rick Dempsey, the scrappy but light-hitting catcher, emerged in this Series as the batting star, driving in one run in that win with a double.

Moving to Philadelphia, Baltimore triumphed in Game 3 by a 3–2 score, and came away with another one-run win in Game 4, 5–4. It was a Series filled with good pitching and key hits by players like Dempsey and second baseman Rich Dauer, who had three hits to lead the Game 4 victory. But in Game 5, Murray, who had gone 2 for 16 in the Series, broke out with two home runs, and Scott McGregor pitched a five-hitter for a 5–0 win and Baltimore's third World Series championship.

From 1966 to 1983, the Orioles won three World Series championships and six pennants, and were always in the hunt to appear in the playoffs. There was no reason, with the likes of such young stars like Murray, Ripken, and Boddicker, that it would not continue after 1983. But owner Edward Bennett Williams wasn't a big fan of the Oriole Way—player development—which had served his team well in the first few years of his ownership. He wanted to take advantage of free agency, and had stars in his eyes. They would blind the franchise for years to come.

Losing the Oriole Way

The end came in 1984, and it was over before it started. The Detroit Tigers, who had finished strong in 1983, got off to a remarkable—and insurmountable—35–5 start, and the pennant race was over after 40 games.

"We thought coming back in 1984 that we would win it again," Rich Dauer said. "But the Tigers got off to that great start and all of a sudden, instead of going out there and playing like we were in 1983, we were chasing and chasing right out of the box, and we always got off to bad starts in April."

They did get off to a bad start, going 4–12, and wound up finishing fifth in the American League East that season, even though they won 85 games. That might have been good enough for most teams, but not the Orioles. It was their lowest win total in 17 years. They finished 19 games behind the Tigers.

Orioles fans knew it was the end of an era when Jim Palmer, at the age of 38, was released on May 17 after going 0–3. Ken Singleton and Al Bumbry soon followed. But fans felt good about the fact that owner Edward Bennett Williams said he wasn't going to simply sit still and let the franchise fall apart. "I should have followed my instincts and made changes," he told reporters. "Instead, because we were World Champs, I decided not to tinker. There were obvious changes that should have been made."

But the way he went about making changes turned out to be disastrous for the Orioles. Instead of building through the farm system, Williams became infatuated with free agency and spent millions on players like outfielder Fred Lynn, a brilliant but infamously injury-prone player; Lee Lacy, a moody outfielder who, at the age of 37, had

TRIVIA

Who was the first president of the United States to watch an Orioles game?

Answers to the trivia questions are on pages 165–166.

seen better days; and others. The chemistry the franchise had created was being eaten away.

Fifth place was not where Williams wanted his team to finish, and when it appeared his club was heading in the same direction in 1985 with a record of 29–26, manager Joe Altobelli was fired. It was done in sloppy fashion, with the media informed about the move before the manager. "I was fired through the grapevine, which I didn't like at all," Altobelli said.

Altobelli was never a Williams choice, though. He was the compromise between general manager Hank Peters and Williams when the two disagreed on a replacement for Earl Weaver when the little general retired after the 1982 season. Williams liked stars. He was the one who brought Vince Lombardi to Washington to coach the Redskins, and then eventually hired George Allen to replace Lombardi after the Hall of Fame coach passed away. So when Altobelli was fired, Williams brought in a star to replace him—a familiar star, the man Altobelli replaced, Earl Weaver. It was suspected that all along, Weaver, who had wanted Cal Ripken Sr. to replace him when he retired, was a confidant of Williams; during the time Altobelli managed the team, there was suspicion that Weaver was undermining Altobelli. "Somebody was talking to Williams," Altobelli said. "I don't know who."

Weaver didn't do any better than Altobelli for the remainder of the 1985 season. After Ripken Sr. managed one game on an interim basis, Weaver took over, and his team went 53–52 for an overall mark of 83–78 and a fourth-place finish in the division.

Eddie Murray had an outstanding season, slamming 31 home runs, driving in 124 runs, and scoring 111 runs, and the combination of Murray and Cal Ripken Jr., who hit 26 home runs, drove in 110 runs, and scored 116 runs, made for a powerful one-two punch in the lineup. Murray was in his prime, and Ripken was in just his fourth full season, so there was every reason to remain optimistic. But little did anyone know that Cal Ripken Jr. would be the final fruit from the Orioles player development tree for more than 20 years. The franchise would not bring up a successful position player from the minor league system until second baseman Brian Roberts in 2003.

There was also optimism going into the 1986 season, because Orioles fans had so much faith in Weaver. That is what made the year such a disappointment. It turned out to be the worst season by an Orioles team since 1956, with a 73–89 record, 22½ games out of first place behind the Boston Red Sox, and a seventh-place finish.

"Everything broke down," Weaver said. "The 0-for-4's, the left on bases, the pitchers allowing all those home runs. It just added up."

Murray had a down year, hitting 17 home runs and driving in just 84 runs. They had just one starter—Mike Boddicker—with a

Jim Palmer, here in 1968, spent his entire career with the Orioles. He ended his career in 1984 after 268 career wins.

Reliever Don Aase is the only Oriole to lose both games of a doubleheader, swept by the Oakland Athletics in August 1986. It was one of two consecutive doubleheader losses for Baltimore, which wound up losing 42 of its last 56 games that season.

winning record, going 14–12. Their anchor, Mike Flanagan, went just 7–11, and the man who caught these outstanding Orioles pitches for so many years—Rick Dempsey—became a free agent after the season and signed with Cleveland.

The sum of that breakdown was a second retirement by Weaver—this one not nearly as glorious. But this time Weaver's right-hand man would finally get his chance at managing a major league team. Cal Ripken Sr. was named manager of the Orioles for the 1987 season. Ripken had been a mainstay in the Orioles system since 1957, as a minor league coach and manager, and then for nine years as the third-base coach for the major league club. He was the favorite of the players for the job, and the fans as well, as the Ripken family had become the first family of baseball in Baltimore, with the rise of Cal Jr. as an All-Star shortstop, and the entry in 1987 of his brother, second baseman Billy Ripken. So Cal Sr. would be managing both of his sons, a first in Major League Baseball history. It would officially happen on July 11, in a 2–1 loss to the Minnesota Twins.

It seemed like a dream come true, but it would turn into a nightmare for the Ripken family. The team finished with a 67–95 record, mostly due in part to the Orioles pitchers getting old—Flanagan and Scott McGregor combined for a 5–13 record and were near the end of their careers—with no young pitchers from the farm system to replace them. And there was one particularly difficult moment for the Ripkens when Cal Sr., as manager, sat down Cal Jr., who had played every inning of every game since 1982, to break his consecutive inning streak at 8,243 innings. Senior replaced his son at shortstop with Ron Washington on September 14 in the eighth inning of an 18–3 loss to the Toronto Blue Jays. It was Ripken's 908th consecutive game. It would be 11

TRIVIA

How did the Baltimore Orioles get their name?

Answers to the trivia questions are on pages 165–166.

more years before the consecutive-game streak that defined Ripken's career would end.

It should have come as no surprise, though, that Cal Sr. would be the one to sit his son down, even against Junior's wishes. He had a reputation for being a tough baseball man who loved the game, and taught his sons to respect the game. When asked after he took over as manager how he would handle managing his son, Senior said, "They're all my sons, all 25 players, and I'll treat them the same."

Edward Bennett Williams, though, wasn't particularly enamored with the family novelty after two straight losing seasons. He was angry, and heads were about to roll. Williams fired general manager Hank Peters. He also tapped Frank Robinson, who had joined the Orioles coaching staff the year before, as the owner's special assistant. The writing was on the wall with that move, but no one thought it would result in such a drastic change so soon.

Why and Why Not?

Hope springs eternal on Opening Day. Everyone believes championships are possible. Then as the season goes on, various teams find out that it isn't their year, that they aren't very good, and there won't be any miracle championship season.

The 1988 Baltimore Orioles found out very quickly that there would be no miracles for them. Nightmares, yes. Miracles, no.

The nightmare began with a 12–0 loss to the Milwaukee Brewers on Opening Day at Memorial Stadium. It was an embarrassing loss for manager Cal Ripken Sr. There would be more, but not many more, because owner Edward Bennett Williams wouldn't need much to make a change he was chomping at the bit to make.

They lost again to the Brewers 3–1. They played the Cleveland Indians next, and were shut out 3–0, pummeled 12–1, and lost the series finale 6–3. After a 7–2 defeat at the hands of the Indians—their sixth straight loss—Williams pulled the trigger and unceremoniously fired the beloved Ripken Sr. the next day. It was one of the lower moments in the history of the franchise, but not the lowest the Orioles would sink to in 1988. They didn't know what low was yet, but it was coming.

Williams replaced Senior with the manager he had wanted all along, Orioles legend Frank Robinson. The change resulted in a 6–1 loss to the Kansas City Royals before a crowd of just 11,000 at Memorial Stadium, and now Baltimore had lost all seven games of the 1988 season and had been outscored 49–8 during those losses.

Everyone figured it couldn't get worse, but it did. There was a 9–3 loss to the Royals, followed by a particularly embarrassing 4–3 loss to Kansas City that saw the Orioles commit three errors and

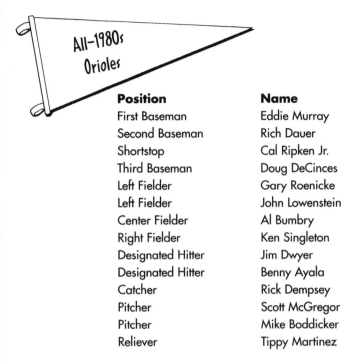

All-1980s
Orioles

Position	Name
First Baseman	Eddie Murray
Second Baseman	Rich Dauer
Shortstop	Cal Ripken Jr.
Third Baseman	Doug DeCinces
Left Fielder	Gary Roenicke
Left Fielder	John Lowenstein
Center Fielder	Al Bumbry
Right Fielder	Ken Singleton
Designated Hitter	Jim Dwyer
Designated Hitter	Benny Ayala
Catcher	Rick Dempsey
Pitcher	Scott McGregor
Pitcher	Mike Boddicker
Reliever	Tippy Martinez

their pitchers two balks—although every loss at this point, with a record of 0–9, was particularly embarrassing.

But when you keep losing, at some point it goes from embarrassing to bizarrely entertaining. That doesn't necessarily happen when you lose your 10th straight game (3–2) to the Indians, or your 11th straight game (1–0) to the Indians, or even the 12th straight game, a 4–1 loss to Cleveland. But when you lose your 13th straight, you tie the record for most consecutive losses to open the season, taking your place with such hapless teams as the 1904 Washington Senators and the 1920 Detroit Tigers, and losing starts to take on a different life. And then, when the 14th-straight loss sets the record, suddenly the whole world is watching.

The Orioles made the cover of *Sports Illustrated*. President Ronald Reagan called after their 18th-straight loss to offer words of encouragement, and thousands of telegrams and messages were arriving at Memorial Stadium to show their support for the team that couldn't win. A Baltimore disc jockey vowed to stay on the air until the Orioles won.

TRIVIA

Who was the Orioles' Opening Day opponent for the 1991 season opener, the final one at Memorial Stadium?

Answers to the trivia questions are on pages 165–166.

Finally, after setting the American League record for consecutive losses with their 21st straight defeat, this one a 4–2 loss to the Minnesota Twins, the Orioles finally stunned the world with a 9–0 win over the White Sox in Chicago. They lost two more and returned home to Baltimore with a 1–23 record, yet more than 50,000 Orioles fans filled the stands at Memorial Stadium on "Fantastic Fans" night to support their home team. And they were rewarded with the announcement that the club had reached an agreement with the State of Maryland for a 30-year lease for a new ballpark, to be built near Baltimore's successful Inner Harbor, in what was known as the Camden area of the city. Governor William Donald Schaefer and owner Edward Bennett Williams made the announcement together. Three months later, Williams lost his long struggle with cancer and passed on. The Orioles would finish that season with a 54–107 record. The novelty of the losing streak had been replaced by despair and uncertainty, fueled by the new owner, Eli Jacobs, who was the mirror opposite of Williams, reclusive and tight-fisted. Then there was the news that Eddie Murray had been traded to the Los Angeles Dodgers in the off-season for three players who would never amount to anything for the Orioles—shortstop Juan Bell and pitchers Brian Holton and Ken Howell.

Murray had become one of the greatest players in franchise history in the 12 years he had been there, leading in home runs with 333 and second to Brooks Robinson in RBIs with 1,190, and a .295 career batting average. But his moodiness and laid-back style on the field had made him a target of fans and writers who were frustrated with the continued ineptness of this once-proud franchise, and he wanted out. So the 1989 season began with little hope for success. That's why they play the games, though.

What happened in 1989 was perhaps as satisfying as any season Orioles fans have ever witnessed. A team around Cal Ripken that consisted primarily of young talent and veteran journeymen who had no business in a pennant race found itself battling the Toronto

Blue Jays right up to the final weekend of the season for the 1989 American League East division title before losing the series in Toronto that weekend. It was known as the "Why Not" team, as in "Why Not Us?" which, based on preseason predictions, seemed nearly impossible. They had a starting pitching staff that had only two pitchers with winning records—Jeff Ballard at 18–8 and Bob Milacki at 14–12. They had just two hitters with more than 20 home runs—Mickey Tettleton with 26 and Ripken with 21, and only Ripken had driven in more than 90 runs, with 93 RBIs. Yet they won 89 games, and manager Frank Robinson, who had suffered through nearly all of that losing streak the year before, was rewarded with AL Manager of the Year honors.

Mickey Tettleton provided surprising power at catcher for the equally surprising 1989 Orioles, who finished only two games out of first place after losing 107 games the year before.

By the
NUMBERS

7—The number of spring training homes for the Orioles. They started in Yuma, Arizona, in 1954, then moved to Daytona, Florida, in 1955, and to Scottsdale in Arizona from 1956 to 1958. They went to Miami in 1959, where they stayed until 1991. From there, it was Sarasota, St. Petersburg, and their current home in Fort Lauderdale.

Baseball, which has become so consistent in Baltimore, was a roller coaster for Orioles fans, with dramatic rises and falls—from 54 wins in 1988 to 89 wins in 1989 and back to 76–85 in 1990. There was little to root for that year, save for the promise that their number-one draft choice that season, 6'7" pitcher Ben McDonald, had shown in his starting debut, a 2–0 shutout win over the Chicago White Sox, and that Ripken had passed Everett Scott during the season to move into second place for consecutive games at 1,411, with only Lou Gehrig ahead of him now.

It appeared that the Jacobs ownership, with team president Larry Lucchino (a partial owner held over from the Williams administration), and general manager Roland Hemond, were ready for the Orioles to take a big step back toward respectability when, on January 10, 1991, they traded three prospects for one of the most feared sluggers in the National League—Houston Astros first baseman Glenn Davis, who had hit 164 home runs from 1985 to 1990 while playing in the spacious Astrodome. It seemed like a great deal for Baltimore, but it would turn out to be the worst trade in franchise history.

Davis became the poster boy for the disabled list, with a series of back problems and other injuries. He played in just 49 games in 1991 and 106 in 1992. By the time he was healthy again in 1993, he just couldn't play anymore, hitting just .177 with one home run in 30 games. He would be released.

The players the Orioles gave up for Davis? Pitchers Pete Harnisch, Curt Schilling, and Steve Finley, all of whom would go on to become All-Stars, and Finley and Schilling in particular having outstanding and long major league careers.

Without the benefit of the expected offense from Davis, the Orioles struggled in 1991—their last season at Memorial Stadium—and, after a

13–24 start, Frank Robinson was removed as manager and took a job in the front office as an assistant general manager. He was replaced by first-base coach Johnny Oates, a former Orioles catcher, who went on to lead the team to an overall mark of 67–95. The season finale was a memorable one, as a sold-out crowd said good-bye to Memorial Stadium. After the game ended many of the past Orioles greats came out on the field to take their places at their respective positions— Brooks Robinson, Paul Blair, Gene Woodling, and so many others. And in a ceremony to mark the transition from old to new, home plate was removed from Memorial Stadium and taken down to be placed at the new home of the Baltimore Orioles—Camden Yards.

Camden Yards

Rick Sutcliffe was a veteran pitcher in demand as a free agent after the 1991 season, not just for his pitching but for his clubhouse presence. He would be considered an asset for any team, and had a group of teams to chose from. You might think that the team that won just 67 games the year before would not be high on his list.

But when Sutcliffe came to Baltimore and took a tour of the new ballpark he was sold. "He [Sutcliffe] told his agent that we were taking advantage of them, that they couldn't say no after seeing this place," general manager Roland Hemond said. "That was his reaction to the beauty of Camden Yards."

Appropriately enough, Sutcliffe would start the first game at the new ballpark on Opening Day in 1992 and beat the Cleveland Indians by the score of 2–0 before a raucous and proud sold-out crowd that embraced the new ballpark.

Camden Yards changed not just baseball, but the entire landscape of professional sports. Its retro-style design—incorporating the intimate feeling and architecture of the smaller, older, baseball-only parks with modern amenities such as numerous luxury boxes, spacious walkways, and festivities beyond the field—has been the blueprint for nearly every stadium built since.

"Camden Yards has changed the thinking of stadium construction," said former Maryland governor William Donald Schaefer, who, using lottery funds, helped push through legislation for the construction of Camden Yards. "The thinking now is how can we benefit the city?"

Ironically, it was the success of Camden Yards and its impact on the continued development in and around Baltimore's Inner Harbor that influenced the decision to put the ballpark of the Orioles' rival, the Washington Nationals, in southeast Washington near the water—the Anacostia River—to revitalize that neighborhood.

But it almost didn't happen. The architects that are so renowned now for their ballpark design—Helmuth, Obata & Kassabaum (HOK)—wanted to build a ballpark in Baltimore that was a replica of the facility they had designed and opened just a year before Camden Yards would open its doors. But the new Comiskey Park in Chicago had no intimacy, sterile surroundings, and an upper level that gave fans vertigo.

But there was one figure through the entire political, baseball, and design process—Orioles team president Larry Lucchino—who had a vision of what Camden Yards would be like: a traditional old ballpark with modern touches. He made his stance emphatically when the architects brought him a very expensive model of a new Comiskey and proposed building a similar ballpark in Baltimore. "We just ripped one

Camden Yards became the new home of the Orioles in 1992. It was an immediately successful change that had a profound effect on the economics of baseball.

TOP 10

Biggest Crowds in Camden Yards History

	Crowd	Opponent	Date
1.	49,828	Boston Red Sox	July 10, 2005
2.	49,696	New York Yankees	June 22, 2004
3.	49,549	Philadelphia Phillies	June 28, 2003
4.	49,334	Boston Red Sox	August 2, 2003
5.	49,331	Boston Red Sox	July 9, 2005
6.	49,174	Boston Red Sox	July 8, 2005
7.	49,072	Boston Red Sox	July 7, 2001
8.	49,013	Atlanta Braves	July 15, 2000
9.	49,004	Colorado Rockies	June 17, 2005
10.	48,937	Philadelphia Phillies	June 28, 2002

piece of it up after another," Lucchino said. "We said, 'We don't want this, we don't want that.' One of the architects said, 'Larry, do you have any idea how much these models cost?' I said, 'No, but we're trying to make a point here.'"

It was a historic point, and the world got to see the future of sports on April 6, 1992, when Camden Yards opened. It had a distinctive look with the old and the new, with the Baltimore skyline in view and the signature feature of the ballpark—the remarkable B&O Warehouse out past right field. The 1,016-foot-long structure, which some officials in the design process initially wanted to tear down, is the longest building on the East Coast and now houses the Orioles offices, among other businesses, after a $20 million renovation. No one has ever hit the warehouse with a home run in a regular-season game, though Ken Griffey hit it during a home-run hitting contest when Baltimore hosted the 1993 All-Star Game.

The warehouse stands in front of Eutaw Street, a walkway before the seats and the building that serves as a promenade of sorts, featuring various food stands. The most notable may be "Boog's Barbecue," the famous barbecue stand named for former Orioles first baseman Boog Powell, who greeted fans as they lined up to get a Boog's sandwich.

Just outside Eutaw Street, at the north end of the warehouse, are the monuments honoring the retired Orioles numbers—Brooks Robinson (5), Jim Palmer (22), Frank Robinson (20), Earl Weaver (4), and Eddie Murray (33).

The first pitch on Opening Day against the Indians was thrown by Sutcliffe at 3:20 PM. The first batter was center fielder Kenny Lofton, who flied out to right fielder Joe Orsulak. Indians first baseman Paul Sorrento got the first hit, a single to left-center field, with one out in the top of the second inning. Ironically, the first Orioles hit in Camden Yards came off the bat of Glenn Davis, the huge bust for the Orioles who came over in the franchise-crippling trade with the Houston Astros the year before. The first Orioles run was scored in the bottom of the fifth inning, when Sam Horn walked, went to second base on a single by Leo Gomez, and scored on a double by Chris Hoiles—the first Orioles RBI at Camden Yards. Two days later, Sorrento hit the first home run at the new ballpark off Bob Milacki, and the day after that, Mike Devereaux hit the first Orioles home run there.

Every home game in that 1992 season would be a sellout in Baltimore, and those sellouts would continue for every game for six years—44,000 fans, 81 times a year. It was a remarkable response for a fan base that had loved the Orioles' old ballpark, Memorial Stadium, and that valued tradition. Perhaps the greatest seal of approval came from Cal Ripken Jr., who had grown up in the Orioles family and was the face of the franchise.

"I was worried that when we went to Camden Yards we would lose the old Orioles history, the feeling of playing in a place that was special for baseball," Ripken said. "But when we got on the field at Camden Yards and started playing there, it seemed like it was a place where baseball had been played before. Intellectually, you knew it was brand new and no baseball had been played there until we got there. But when you walked into the place it was a ballpark. It represented so many things and brought up some deep feelings about the game."

It seemed to transform the entire franchise. The Orioles won two of the first three games against Cleveland in that opening series. After going on the road and losing four out of five, they came back to Camden Yards and swept the Detroit Tigers in four games. They

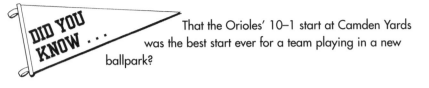

That the Orioles' 10–1 start at Camden Yards was the best start ever for a team playing in a new ballpark?

went on to win the next three against the Kansas City Royals on the road for a seven-game winning streak. They would win 10 of their first 11 games at the new ballpark, the best start ever for a team playing in a new home. However, the stadium was not so kind to the Orioles the rest of the season, as they went 33–37 in their remaining home games to finish with a 43–38 home mark.

Still, the Orioles went from a 67–95 team to a winning club that competed with the Toronto Blue Jays for the American League East title down to the final weeks of the season, finishing with an 89–73 record, good for third place in the division and just seven games out from first. And a new group of Orioles emerged as stars for the franchise—outfielder Brady Anderson had a breakout year, with 21 home runs, 80 RBIs, 100 runs scored, 53 stolen bases, and a .271 batting average as the leadoff hitter. He would go on to become one of the favorite players in franchise history, and is among the franchise leaders in numerous categories, including fourth in runs scored (1,044), fourth in hits (1,614), fifth in doubles (329), and first in stolen bases (307) before leaving after the 2001 season. Mike Mussina became the staff ace in just his second season, posting an 18–5 record with a 2.54 ERA. He would go on to become one of the all-time best pitchers in a franchise rich with pitching—second in strikeouts (1,535) and third in wins (147) before leaving after the 2000 season.

These were among the players who would be the cornerstone of the future team anchored by Cal Ripken, and would represent the Orioles in a total of eight All-Star Games among them. Anderson played in the 1992 All-Star Game in San Diego. Mussina, along with Ripken, would be fortunate enough to represent the Orioles when Baltimore and Camden Yards hosted the 1993 All-Star Game. Mussina did not appear in the game, yet he would have a historic impact that continues to this day.

All-Stars and Angelos

By the start of the 1993 season, Camden Yards had become the crown jewel of baseball, capturing national headlines for its design and success in selling out game after game. Others would follow soon—Jacobs Field in Cleveland and The Ballpark in Arlington, Texas, in 1994—but going into its second season, Camden Yards stood alone as the first of the new generation of retro ballparks, and it would have a chance to strut its stuff by hosting the 1993 All-Star Game.

Orioles fans would have a chance to root for two of their own on the team—Cal Ripken, elected by the fans, and Mike Mussina, selected by the American League skipper Cito Gaston, the manager of the 1992 World Champion Toronto Blue Jays. The Blue Jays were rising fast on the enemies list of Orioles fans.

The rivalry between the Blue Jays and Orioles took root in the 1989 "Why Not" season in Baltimore, when a team of no-names and journeymen battled Toronto for the division title up to the last weekend of the season. It heated up when the Orioles fielded a competitive team in 1992 and again battled the Blue Jays for much of the season, and was in full force again in 1993, with the Orioles just one and a half games behind the Blue Jays before the All-Star break.

So Gaston ratcheted it up a notch when he added four of his Blue Jays players to the three already voted in by the fans, giving Toronto 25 percent of the AL roster. "I don't have to apologize to anybody," Gaston said. "Anyway, I'm used to being criticized. It happens all the time in Toronto."

But what would happen in Baltimore to Gaston never happened in Toronto.

TRIVIA

How many broadcasters who spent time with the Orioles have been inducted into the Hall of Fame?

Answers to the trivia questions are on pages 165–166.

With the AL leading 9–3 in the eighth inning, most of Gaston's pitchers had been used, save for three—Minnesota's Rick Aguilera, Gaston's closer, Duane Ward, and the hometown favorite, Mussina. And fans were starting to grouse about not seeing their star pitcher take the mound at a game in his home ballpark. In the eighth inning, Gaston brought in Aguilera. Everyone expected Gaston to put Mussina in, with a six-run lead, to pitch at some point before the game ended. But he called on Ward to come in for the ninth inning, and a chorus of boos greeted the decision. Then things got crazy.

Mussina got up to warm up in the bullpen on his own, and the Jumbotron ballpark screen showed him warming up. The crowd chanted for Mussina. But Gaston had not told Mussina to warm up, and Mussina claimed he was just getting his work in for his next start. Still, he must have known his act would create an uproar, and it did just that, and created one of the most bizarre endings in the history of the All-Star Game.

The AL won 9–3, yet the stadium was filled with thunderous boos as the players left the field, and then they cheered Mussina as he walked in from the bullpen. The pitcher acknowledged the cheers but could not have imagined that he set off a controversy that would continue for days, and, according to some observers, has affected the All-Star Game to this day.

All of the postgame questions were related to Gaston's failure to use Mussina and Mussina's warm-up act. Orioles officials were furious. "Why you can't get Mike Mussina in a 9–3 game is beyond me," general manager Roland Hemond said. "I don't care what your explanation is. If you say you have to save him for extra innings, you don't have any faith in Duane Ward."

The next day, the controversy raged. It was national news, and Gaston became public enemy number one in Baltimore. "Cito Gaston insulted the city of Baltimore," sports talk show host Jeff Rimer said, and fans flooded the talk shows with angry criticisms of the Blue Jays

Mike Mussina, here beating the Tigers in 1998, was the Orioles' ace for nine seasons, collecting 147 wins in a Baltimore uniform, including a league-leading 19 in 1995.

TRIVIA

Which future minor league player participated in the Celebrity Home Run Challenge at the All-Star Game workout at Camden Yards in 1993?

Answers to the trivia questions are on pages 165–166.

manager. It got ugly as time wore on, with charges of racial overtones. Fan began walking around Baltimore with "Cito Sucks" T-shirts, and when the Blue Jays came to town after that, Gaston said he feared for his safety as well as the safety of his players. "There are a lot of weird people in the world," Gaston said. "Maybe I'll have a shotgun strapped to my leg."

Before that, though, the Orioles would travel to Toronto two weeks after the All-Star Game. Though the bad feelings lingered, Mussina apologized to Gaston by telephone from manager Johnny Oates's office in the visiting clubhouse, even though Gaston was just across the field at Sky Dome in the home clubhouse. "I talked to him, and as far as I'm concerned, it's settled," Mussina said.

But it was never truly settled. The bad feelings in Baltimore remained until Gaston was out of baseball. And at the 2006 All-Star Game in Pittsburgh, when asked about the use of pitchers by All-Star Game managers and how it led to the 2002 All-Star Game tie in Milwaukee, commissioner Bud Selig said he believed that the effort by managers to get as many players in the game as possible, even at the expense of winning the game, was a direct result of what happened to Gaston in Baltimore in 1993.

The Orioles stayed in the division hunt with the Blue Jays until the final weeks of the season, and finished in a tie for third place with an 85–77 record. But as the season was winding down, all eyes were not on the field, but instead on a hot New York courtroom in August, where the future of the Orioles franchise was being decided.

Team owner Eli Jacobs was on the verge of bankruptcy, and team president Larry Lucchino, in a partnership with Cincinnati businessman William DeWitt, were set to buy the Orioles from Jacobs for $140 million. But Jacobs's creditors forced him into bankruptcy before the deal could be made, and the team was put up for auction in bankruptcy court. Enter former Baltimore city councilman, political power broker, and powerful attorney Peter Angelos, who had made a fortune litigating asbestos cases against manufacturers.

Angelos claimed that the ownership group that included DeWitt, an out-of-town owner, would raise the possibility of the franchise being relocated, even though the team was locked into a 30-year lease at Camden Yards, and said his bid was the best chance for local ownership. At the last minute, before a bankruptcy auction in New York, DeWitt agreed to join up with Angelos, and they outbid art dealer Jeffrey Loria (who, six years later, would buy the Montreal Expos and then be involved in a three-franchise deal in 2002 that would land him the Florida Marlins), and former NFL tight end Jean Fugett, the chief executive officer of the Beatrice Corporation, with a record $173 million bid.

Angelos said he didn't think he would be a hands-on owner. "I can be pretty detached," he said.

Nothing could have been further from the truth. Angelos and his two young sons, John and Lou, would be involved in nearly all of the personnel decisions on the franchise in their early years of owner-ship. Initially, his impact was a positive one. He was willing to spend money to bring in free agents like first baseman Rafael Palmeiro, closer Lee Smith, and starting pitcher Sid Fernandez. The Orioles were competing with the New York Yankees for the division title in 1994, when, in second place with a 63–49 record, the season came to an end on August 11. Players went on strike in the most bitter labor dispute in the history of professional sports, a strike that led to the cancellation of the playoffs and World Series. The dispute went on into the early part of 1995, and Angelos gained national praise when he refused to go along with his fellow owners and assemble a replacement team in spring training. A fight between Angelos and his fellow owners was averted when a federal court ruled against the owners just before Opening Day, forcing them to abide by the terms of the previous contract. And, as the 1995 season began, albeit delayed several weeks before play could begin, Camden Yards would again become the center of the baseball universe, which was spin-ning out of control, as fans remained angry over the strike. An Oriole would bring them back, not just to Camden Yards, but back to the attraction of the game. Cal Ripken showed up every day to play. It would be baseball's saving grace.

Eddie Murray

Since player development and the farm system was behind so much of the success of the Baltimore Orioles, its fans paid close attention to the progress of young players at the organization's various minor league stops, from Bluefield, West Virginia, to Rochester, New York.

So when Eddie Murray arrived as a major leaguer in Baltimore in 1977, he was already touted as the franchise's next big star, and he heard the chant, "Ed-die! Ed-die!" when he first took the field.

He was unnerved by it.

"When you come out of the minors and get into a major league uniform and all of a sudden hear that," Murray said, recalling his 1977 debut as a highly trumpeted Baltimore rookie, "it's awesome. It made me uncomfortable. But I learned to deal with it, so I could go out and do my job."

That was Eddie Murray in a nutshell—doing his job in spite of the attention.

Murray came from a baseball family in a baseball world, born in Los Angeles and growing up in South Central, playing on a high school team that included future Hall of Fame shortstop Ozzie Smith. His three brothers all played baseball, and Rich would also make the major leagues. But Eddie Murray was the one who emerged as one of the most consistent run producers of his time, driving in 75 runs or more per year from the time he made his debut in 1977 through 1996, just one year short of his entire major league career; Murray stepped down in 1997. And he was far from one-dimensional, having won three Gold Glove awards at first base.

Along the way, he carved a place for himself on the Mount Rushmore of baseball hitting, joining Hank Aaron and Willie Mays as the only ones—without the taint of a positive steroid drug test (like Rafael Palmeiro)—with 500 home runs and 3,000 hits. Murray retired with 504 career home runs, 3,255 hits, and 1,917 RBIs, which put him at eighth in the history of the game.

He had to be that good, because Murray chose the path of most resistance to the pressures of publicity throughout much of his major league career by refusing to deal with the press. He became increasingly distrustful of reporters after a conflict with a New York

One of the best switch hitters of all time, Eddie Murray spent the first 12 years of his Hall of Fame career in an Orioles uniform. Here he hits career home run number 500 against the Tigers on September 6, 1996.

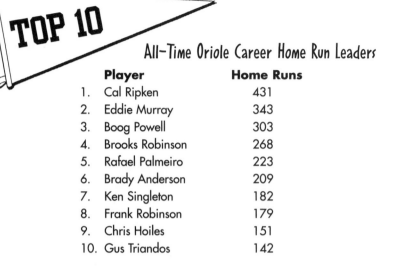

TOP 10

All-Time Oriole Career Home Run Leaders

Player	Home Runs
1. Cal Ripken	431
2. Eddie Murray	343
3. Boog Powell	303
4. Brooks Robinson	268
5. Rafael Palmeiro	223
6. Brady Anderson	209
7. Ken Singleton	182
8. Frank Robinson	179
9. Chris Hoiles	151
10. Gus Triandos	142

columnist early in his career. "There were some things that were done that were awful and rotten," Murray said, who used the incident to conduct a boycott of the media. "I couldn't win that fight," he said. "It's not a level playing field. You can't pretend that it is."

But that fight also illustrates what an amazing player he was, because while his reputation suffered in the press, many of his teammates said he was the greatest leader and friend they had. When Cal Ripken broke Lou Gehrig's consecutive-game record of 2,130 games in 1995, he thanked four people—his father, his mother, his wife, and Murray, who had not been Ripken's teammate since 1988. "I thank him for his example and his friendship," Ripken said.

When Murray came up to the Orioles in 1977, he certainly justified the chants from fans. He appeared in 160 games his rookie season, batting a solid .283 with 27 home runs, 81 runs scored, and 88 RBIs, and won the American League's Rookie of the Year award.

Over each of the next three seasons, Murray improved his production, increasing his batting average, RBIs, and runs scored each year. In 1979, he helped the Orioles to an AL pennant, batting .300 with 32 home runs and 116 RBIs. Three years later, when he drove in 110 runs, it was the first of four straight seasons with 100 or more RBIs.

Murray batted .300 or better in four out of five seasons during the first half of the 1980s. He also slugged better than .500 six years in a row. In 1984, he showed a keen eye at the plate by leading the AL with a .415 on-base percentage and 107 walks.

In 1983 he led the Orioles in RBIs with 111 and achieved a career high of 33 home runs. He struggled in the World Series against the Philadelphia Phillies until the fifth game, when he blasted two mammoth home runs to help Baltimore clinch its first World Series championship since 1970.

But there was a new star on the field in Ripken, and as the Orioles began bringing in free agents who didn't fit in with the Oriole way, the team began struggling. After three straight losing seasons, including the 21-game losing streak in the 107-loss 1988 season, fans began targeting Murray for the team's woes, and worse, he was criticized in the press by owner Edward Bennett Williams.

It resulted in the team being forced to make one of the worst trades in club history, dealing Murray after the 1988 season to the Los Angeles Dodgers for shortstop Juan Bell and pitchers Brian Holton and Ken Howell—none of whom were heard of for much longer.

Murray continued to be a strong run producer and team leader with the Dodgers, the New York Mets, and then the Cleveland Indians before getting a chance, under new owner Peter Angelos, to come home in July 1996 to Baltimore as the designated hitter in a trade that helped the Orioles go on to win the AL wild card and make the playoffs for the first time since 1983.

He retired in 1997 and would continue to work as a coach for the Orioles and Indians, and currently with the Dodgers. His number (33) has been retired by the Orioles. And Murray, despite his battles with writers, was elected to the National Baseball Hall of Fame in 2003. Being consistent, he fired one final shot as the press.

Murray devoted part of his speech to Ted Williams who, during his Hall of Fame induction in 1966, had said, "I must have earned this. I know I didn't win it with my friendship with the writers."

TRIVIA

How many American League Most Valuable Player awards did Eddie Murray win?

Answers to the trivia questions are on pages 165–166.

"In that way," Murray said, "I'm proud to be in his company."

And then he explained why he shunned the spotlight, and also illustrated why he was so admired by his teammates.

"To me, words focused on the individual," Murray said. "It had nothing to do with how you hit or how you played the game. Baseball is a team game. It's not an *I* or a *me* thing. That's what I learned. And that's what I still believe in."

Of course, it ended as it began—Orioles fans in attendance that day in Cooperstown chanting, "Ed-die! Ed-die!"

Davey Comes Home

Peter Angelos wasn't going to sit on his hands and live with the dis-appointment of the 1995 losing season. Heads would roll, and they did. General manager Roland Hemond was fired, as well as manager Phil Regan. This time, Angelos would not make the same mistake twice, though he certainly went about it in an unusual way when he hired their replacements.

He had his newly hired manager recruit the candidate for general manager. But by doing so, the Orioles owner put together an All-Star management team.

First he corrected his mistake in 1995 by hiring Davey Johnson to manage the Orioles, after passing over him initially in favor of Regan, which had turned out to be a huge miscalculation. Then Angelos set his sights on a most unlikely candidate for general manager—former Toronto Blue Jays front office boss Pat Gillick.

Gillick was one of the most successful general managers of his time, having built the Blue Jays from an expansion franchise into a perennial winner that captured two straight World Series champi-onships in 1992 and 1993. He had retired, handing the reins over to his assistant, Gord Ash, and working for the franchise as a consultant. So Angelos put out the word that he would like to consider Gillick—a former Orioles minor league pitcher—to run his team's baseball operations. But Gillick was not particularly interested after he heard horror stories from Hemond and others about the difficulties of working for Angelos and the way he meddled in baseball decisions.

But Johnson, who was close to Gillick—they were former minor league teammates in the Orioles system—convinced Gillick that they could handle the Orioles owner, and that there was an opportunity to

TRIVIA

Who hit the home run that clinched the wild card berth for the Orioles in 1996?

Answers to the trivia questions are on pages 165–166.

go back to the place where they both got their start and help restore the "Oriole Way." So Gillick, like Johnson, agreed to a three-year contract.

Gillick hit the ground running. He signed free agents Roberto Alomar and B.J. Surhoff and pitchers Randy Myers and Kent Mercker. He traded for pitcher David Wells. He let pitchers Kevin Brown and Jamie Moyer leave, as well as Angelos's favorite third baseman, Leo Gomez. But Gillick found out early that Angelos could not be handled and that his tenure there would be marred by the owner's interference.

Gillick was trying to sign pitcher David Cone to a three-year deal, and his main competition was Baltimore's division rival, the New York Yankees, for whom Cone had pitched the previous season. The two teams engaged in a bidding war, but Gillick went to Angelos and said he could get Cone signed if the Orioles owner would be willing to put up another $180,000 for the deal. Angelos refused, Cone signed with the Yankees, and the destiny of both franchises changed with that deal. Cone was the leader of the Yankees' clubhouse and helped set the tone for first-year manager Joe Torre. He was the heart and soul of the franchise in the early days of their 10-year run—with four World Series championships—and he was the one who took the ball in tough situations.

Take him out of that Yankees staff and out of that clubhouse—still in the formative stages of those Torre-guided teams—and put him on the Orioles staff and in their clubhouse (one that was in desperate need of leadership at the time), and there is little doubt who would have won in 1996, and would have what happened beyond that.

"He was a heck of a pitcher and the sort of teammate that would make everybody better," said Jim Palmer, the Hall of Fame pitcher and Orioles analyst, who had a front-row seat to the events that have taken place between the two teams since 1996. "When you take two teams that were pretty equally matched, and at the time the Orioles and the Yankees were, and take a player like that from one team and put him on another, it would have had a significant impact. Everything took off for the Yankees after 1996."

Then again, it also might have been different if it wasn't for a 12-year-old kid named Jeffrey Maier.

The Orioles struggled throughout 1996 with inconsistent performances. They had enough talent to win 88 games and just capture the wild card. They got a lift when former Orioles great Eddie Murray came back to Baltimore in a trade at the end of July to secure the designated hitting position. And Brady Anderson had one of the most remarkable seasons of any leadoff hitter in history, slugging a team-record 50 home runs.

But they went into the playoffs surrounded by the biggest controversy baseball had seen since the strike ended, when, on the last weekend of the season in Toronto, Alomar spit in the face of home-plate umpire John Hirschbeck, setting off a firestorm of national criticism and a threatened walkout by umpires in the postseason.

Former Orioles great Davey Johnson returned to the team in 1996 to lead the Birds to a second- and first-place finish in the American League East.

Davey Johnson never won fewer than 90 games in his first five years as a manager, all with the New York Mets.

Despite the furor, the Orioles managed to defeat the Cleveland Indians in the division playoffs and would face the Yankees in the League Championship Series. In Game 1 at Yankee Stadium, with the Orioles leading 4–3 in the bottom of the eighth inning, Derek Jeter hit a long fly ball to right field that Orioles outfielder Tony Tarasco appeared to be under as he backed up to the wall. But Maier, a kid from Old Tappan, New Jersey, reached out and tried to snatch the ball away before it could land in Tarasco's glove. It was clearly fan interference, but umpire Rich Garcia called it a home run, tying the game at 4–4. The Yankees would go on to win 5–4.

Before the game, Orioles management had met with Yankees management and the umpires to talk about the ground rules at the ballpark, and their number one topic of conversation was fan interference. "It was like it was almost spoken into existence," assistant general manager Kevin Malone said.

Although the Orioles had come back to win Game 2, the air was deflated. The Yankees came back to Baltimore to sweep the Orioles in three straight, thanks to the bat of resurrected formerly disgraced Mets star Darryl Strawberry, who had three huge home runs in the series. The Orioles fell short, but had come close enough to feel positive about their prospects for 1997.

However, a growing tension between Angelos and Johnson would ultimately explode and help destroy the plans to return the franchise to its glory days.

Gillick did not stand pat to assemble the 1997 squad. They did not re-sign Murray, instead bringing back another former Oriole, Maryland native Harold Baines, as the DH. They let Wells go and signed former Blue Jays and Yankees starter Jimmy Key. They signed free agent outfielder Eric Davis, who had retired from baseball because of a variety of injuries, but came back to play for the Reds in 1996 and hit 26 home runs, drove in 83 runs, and stole 23 bases in 129 games. And, in the biggest move, Cal Ripken went from shortstop to third base and was replaced by Mike Bordick.

On the field, things went much more smoothly in 1997, as the Orioles led the AL East from Opening Day to the final game of the season, posting a 98–64 record. But they were hit hard by the news that Davis had been diagnosed with colon cancer in June. Remarkably, following surgery and recovery, Davis would come back in time to play in the postseason.

The Orioles were able to overcome the loss of Davis for much of the season but not the war between Angelos and Johnson. The war came to a head when the manager fined Alomar for failing to make the trip for a midseason exhibition game against their Class AAA team in Rochester, and then putting the $10,000 fine toward a charity administered by Johnson's wife. Angelos—already angry at Johnson because he thought he wasn't respectful enough to the owner and did not put enough time into his job—used this as ammunition to raise the battle to the level where the manager was asking questions going into the playoffs about whether or not he would be fired.

With this tension as the backdrop, the Orioles faced Randy Johnson and the Seattle Mariners in the divisional playoffs and won three out of four to move on and face the Cleveland Indians in the ALCS. The Orioles had upset the defending AL pennant winners in the 1996 playoffs, but this time it was Cleveland that upset the favored Orioles in the ALCS in six games, the devastating blow coming in Game 2, with Baltimore poised to take a 2–0 lead in the series, and in the clinching Game 6—both home runs given up by hard-throwing reliever Armando Benitez.

The Orioles had gone to the playoffs for two straight seasons after failing to see postseason play in 13 years. Yet everyone was waiting to see if Angelos would fire Johnson. He didn't have to. The day Johnson was named AL Manager of the Year, he faxed his resignation to Angelos.

It turned out to be a declaration of despair for the franchise.

The Fall from Grace

Peter Angelos had someone waiting in the wings to replace Davey Johnson for the 1998 season—the pitching coach Angelos had brought on in 1997, Ray Miller, who had been Earl Weaver's pitching coach for many years. Angelos was convinced that Miller, who had failed in a previous stint as manager of the Minnesota Twins, would keep the winning ways going.

It was one of many miscalculations that the Baltimore owner would make. The franchise was about to embark on the worst era of losing and embarrassment since the St. Louis Browns moved to Baltimore in 1954.

Pat Gillick was terribly disappointed that Johnson had quit, and had tried to convince him not to. But he knew that their plan to rebuild the franchise for long-term success would never happen as long as Angelos owned the club, so the general manager would just work out the final year of his three-year contract and then leave at the end of the 1998 season. Angelos—who had come to rely on former Pittsburgh Pirates general manager Syd Thrift as his baseball confidant—would not try to keep him.

Gillick signed outfielder Joe Carter and pitcher Doug Drabek to shore up the roster, and both would be huge disappointments. Carter played in just 84 games and batted .247, with 11 home runs and 34 RBIs. Drabek was 6–11 with a 7.29 ERA in 21 starts. Alomar, also in the final year of his contract, slumped, batting .282 with 14 home runs and 56 RBIs. Rafael Palmeiro had a standout year, hitting 43 home runs and driving in 121 runs. Mussina went 13–10 and spent two stints on the disabled list, and Jimmy Key got married and was never the same.

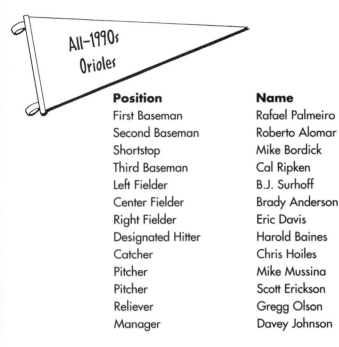

All-1990s
Orioles

Position	Name
First Baseman	Rafael Palmeiro
Second Baseman	Roberto Alomar
Shortstop	Mike Bordick
Third Baseman	Cal Ripken
Left Fielder	B.J. Surhoff
Center Fielder	Brady Anderson
Right Fielder	Eric Davis
Designated Hitter	Harold Baines
Catcher	Chris Hoiles
Pitcher	Mike Mussina
Pitcher	Scott Erickson
Reliever	Gregg Olson
Manager	Davey Johnson

None of the players had much respect for Miller, and all this added up to a 79–83 season and a fourth-place finish in the AL East. Angelos wouldn't sit still for that, and he made a major off-season move that would rank among the worst miscalculations he had ever made.

Gillick left, and so did Alomar and Eric Davis. Attendance dropped for the first time in franchise history, from its record 3.7 million in 1997 to 3.6 million in 1998. Angelos brought in a young, promising baseball man from the Florida Marlins organization named Frank Wren to be his new GM. Then he immediately put the pressure on Wren to sign what had become the prize of the free agent market.

Albert Belle was the most feared hitter in baseball, and he helped lead the Cleveland Indians to the 1995 World Series. He became a free agent and signed a five-year, $55 million contract with the Chicago White Sox, but after two seasons there and a 49-home-run, 152-RBI season in 1997, took advantage of a loophole in his contract and tested the free agent waters again. The Orioles got into a bidding war with the rival Yankees and, unfortunately, came out on top and signed Belle to a five-year, $65 million contract—just one more mis-calculation. As Belle arrived, Palmeiro, who had put in the best five-year span of any player in the history of the Orioles with 182 home runs and 553 RBIs, departed for Texas. People criticized Angelos for letting Palmeiro, a fan favorite, leave. Ironically, the mistake was not in letting him leave, but in bringing him back five years later.

Statistically, Belle had a solid year, hitting 37 home runs and driving in 117 runs, but he was a cancer in the clubhouse and became the target of the wrath of Orioles fans. The franchise suf-fered a severe loss when one of its legendary figures, Cal Ripken Sr., passed away. Wren clashed with Angelos and left after one season, and the team finished with a 78–84 record.

Infielder Melvin Mora, here about to slide into home during a game in 2006, had 27 back-to-back home-run seasons for the Orioles.

The highlight of the year, it turned out, was the Orioles' historic trip in March to Havana, Cuba, to play the Cuban national team. Angelos had arranged an exchange with the Cuban government in which the Orioles would play a game in Havana, and the Cuban team would come to Camden Yards in May. The Orioles won the game in Havana 3–2. The second game may have been the lowlight for the franchise, as the Orioles lost 12–6 in an embarrassing and controversial performance—one protestor who ran on the field was tackled by a Cuban umpire—before their fans.

Angelos pretty much surrendered the pretense of not controlling the baseball decisions for the 2000 season when he made Thrift the vice president of baseball operations and general manager—yet another move to further bury the franchise. Thrift had a reputation throughout baseball as someone who could not be trusted, and agents told their clients to stay away from the Orioles.

Angelos fired Miller and brought in a big name and proven winner, Mike Hargrove, who had been fired by the Indians after leading them to five AL Central division crowns but had failed to deliver a World Series championship with the very talented teams he had. He also failed to deliver much with the very untalented team he had in Baltimore, as the Orioles finished with a 74–88 record for the 2000 season. Thrift presided over the worst fire sale in franchise history when, in the middle of July, he traded Harold Baines, B.J. Surhoff, catcher Charles Johnson, first baseman Will Clark, shortstop Mike Bordick, and reliever Mike Timlin.

"Three years from now, somebody is going to look pretty smart up here," Thrift said, crowing about the young players and prospects he acquired in the trades.

No one looked smart, though. Of the 14 players they acquired, only one turned out to be a legitimate major leaguer, Melvin Mora, and he was a throw-in utility player from the New York Mets—although he has since emerged as an All-Star third baseman for the franchise. Attendance continued its downward spiral, falling to 3.2 million.

While this was happening, the New York Yankees had won four out of five World Series championships.

The 2001 season was not much better, as the Orioles fell from the 70-win class to the dismal 60-win neighborhood where the worst

When Scott Erickson pitched to the Cuban national team in the bottom of the first inning of the Orioles exhibition game in Havana in 1999, he became the first major leaguer to pitch on Cuban soil in 40 years, and his jersey was put on display at the national Baseball Hall of Fame.

teams in baseball reside, with a 63–98 record, the worst since the 1988 losing streak season. Thrift attempted to sign free agents, but when he found that no one was taking, he declared it was as if the Orioles had "confederate money." They were forced into overpaying for mediocre talent, such as David Segui, who signed a four-year $28 million contract and spent most of those four seasons on the disabled list. They were forced to use 18 rookies that year. Two of them—Jay Gibbons and Brian Roberts—would develop into solid major league players, but it would not be enough to fill all the holes of a hemorrhaging organization.

Again, it would be Cal Ripken who would at least take some of the attention away from the team's problems, though it would be the last time. Ripken announced he would retire at the end of the 2001 season, and fans turned out to get their last look at the Oriole legend. Even so, attendance continued to fall to 3 million in their fourth straight losing season. The team held a ceremony for Ripken on the final day of the season, and although the Orioles lost 5–1 to the Red Sox, it was still a moment for the fans to feel good about their team. Those moments were very few.

"Cal became the symbol for the American work ethic and the symbol for the American working man," baseball commissioner Bud Selig said, and former president Bill Clinton called Ripken "the kind of man every father would like his son to grow up to be."

Ripken would be gone in 2002, and so would Mike Mussina, who left after 10 seasons and 147 wins to sign a five-year deal with the Yankees. Also gone was any reason to come to Camden Yards. The Orioles had their fifth straight losing season, with a 67–95 record, and the fans stayed away, as attendance dropped to 2.6 million. Angelos finally fired Thrift and in his place hired two people to run the front office—former Montreal Expos general manager Jim

Beattie and a very familiar face for Baltimore fans, former left-handed Cy Young Award winner and team broadcaster Mike Flanagan. He was one of the most beloved figures in franchise history, but after working for Angelos for several seasons, he had tarnished his image, perhaps forever, with his questionable moves.

They progressed slightly to 71 victories in 2003, but the fans still weren't buying. The number of people who walked through the turnstiles in 2004 was 2.4 million, lower than the strike-shortened season of 1995 and the club's lowest figure since 1988 in Memorial Stadium. Not even trying to cash in on coach Eddie Murray's induction into the Hall of Fame would help.

Flanagan and Beattie wanted to make an impact on the team that would turn the mentality around. Instead, they made a bad situation worse.

Steroids and Shame, but Home Remains

Most observers figured that the front office team of Jim Beattie and Mike Flanagan would do the right thing in their search to replace Mike Hargrove as manager of the Baltimore Orioles and hire longtime and highly respected coach Sam Perlozzo. The Cumberland, Maryland, native had been on the coaching staff since 1996, and had spent four seasons as bench coach. He seemed like the perfect fit.

But Beattie and Flanagan—soon to be derisively called "Beatagan"—stunned everyone when they passed over Perlozzo and hired someone with far less experience who had no connection whatsoever to the Orioles—former New York Met Lee Mazzilli.

He had been a coach on Yankees manager Joe Torre's staff for four seasons, from 2000 to 2003, and had three successful years as a minor league manager, from 1997 to 1999. But he was not considered to be a serious candidate for the Orioles job. Beatagan, though, said Mazzilli was impressive in his interview. To other observers, that assessment was remarkable, because Mazzilli did nothing to impress anyone else—writers, players, or fans.

He would take over a team that had made a number of major free agent moves to bring the club back to respectability, like signing superstar shortstop Miguel Tejada and All-Star catcher Javy Lopez, and bringing back Rafael Palmeiro. All three delivered statistically— Tejada had an MVP-caliber season, hitting 34 home runs and driving in a club-record 150 runs; Lopez batted .316 with 23 home runs and 86 RBIs; and Palmeiro, at the age of 40, hit 23 home runs and drove in 88 runs.

Position	Name
First Baseman	Eddie Murray
Second Baseman	Roberto Alomar
Shortstop	Cal Ripken
Third Baseman	Brooks Robinson
Left Fielder	Brady Anderson
Center Fielder	Paul Blair
Right Fielder	Frank Robinson
Catcher	Rick Dempsey
Pitcher	Jim Palmer
Pitcher	Mike Mussina
Reliever	Gregg Olson
Manager	Earl Weaver

But one free agent they signed did not deliver as expected, and it was the one the Orioles should have known better about. They had traded problematic pitcher Sidney Ponson, who had a 14–6 record, to the San Francisco Giants in the middle of the 2003 season for three pitching prospects, none of whom ever became major league hurlers. It had been the first time that Ponson, who suffered from weight and alcohol problems, had managed to put together a winning season. But since it was a contract year, the team should have been suspect of those numbers. Instead, they signed Ponson to a three-year, $24 million contract, and he reported to camp overweight and out of shape in 2004, and wound up going 11–15 with a 5.30 ERA.

The big names brought some of the fans back, as attendance shot up to 2.7 million. But they saw their seventh-straight losing season, with a 78–84 record—still their most victories since 1999. So it appeared the team was slowly moving in the right direction. It was an illusion, however, as things would never get worse for the Baltimore Orioles than they would in the 2005 season, with unprecedented embarrassments galore.

A former American League MVP, shortstop Miguel Tejada signed with the Orioles as a free agent before the 2004 season. He promptly hit 34 home runs, drove in 150 runs, and was named to the All-Star team.

First there was Ponson, the fat and rich Aruban knight and Orioles pitcher. On Christmas Day 2004, he was arrested in Aruba and charged with assaulting an Aruban judge following a complaint about Ponson's handling of his powerboat. He spent 11 days in jail, but the charges were dropped after he reached a settlement that included restitution, community service, and contributions to local charities on the island. In January 2005, he was charged with driving under the influence in Broward County, Florida. Eight months later, Ponson was arrested for driving under the influence and driving while impaired on southbound Interstate 95 near downtown Baltimore. In September, the Orioles released Ponson and voided his contract, saying that his infractions with the law went against a morals clause in Major League Baseball contracts. On December 12, 2005, Ponson was sentenced to five days in the Baltimore city jail after he was found guilty of driving while impaired. He was also fined $535. He was released from jail on December 19.

That might have been enough, but Ponson was a sideshow compared to what else happened in 2005.

The circus began in the winter when the Orioles brought Chicago Cubs home-run legend Sammy Sosa to Baltimore. Sosa had hit 574 career home runs, but had fallen out of favor in Chicago, and his star was tarnished, first by being caught several years before using a corked bat and then by the suspicions of steroid use. The Orioles traded second baseman/outfielder Jerry Hairston and two minor leaguers for Sosa, and were only obligated to pay $8.85 million of his $17 million salary for 2005, with the Cubs picking up the rest. It was no bargain.

"I gave Chicago everything that I have. It was a beautiful experience for my wife and family," Sosa said. "I had a great time in Chicago, but you have to move on. This is my new house, and I love it."

But there was no love in Baltimore, though the team tried to cash in on Sosa. They put him, Tejada, and Palmeiro on the cover of their 2005 media guide. Two of them would be dragged before Congress in a hearing in March on steroids, prompted by the devastating book by Jose Canseco, and both would deny, in their own way, using steroids, though Sosa's denial was more vague and written for legal purposes. Palmeiro was adamant, and waved his finger at the panel to emphasis his innocence. It was a historic moment, one that would haunt the Orioles franchise.

Sosa would play in just 102 games, sidelined with a variety of injuries, and he hit just 14 home runs and batted .221. He shrank in size before everyone's eyes and literally was told to go home with a few weeks left in the season because his presence was so undesirable.

And even that was not the biggest problem the Orioles had.

TRIVIA

What was the last day of the 2005 season that the Orioles were in first place?

Answers to the trivia questions are on pages 165–166.

After starting the season off with a winning record, and being in first place in the AL East from April to June, the Orioles went 9–28 and fell to 10½ games behind the first-place Boston Red Sox. So they fired Lee Mazzilli and replaced him with the man who many believe should have had the job in the first place, Perlozzo. Mazzilli had long lost the clubhouse, and the players had held a team meeting early in the season to state they would win in spite of their manager, not because of him.

And even that wasn't the biggest problem the team had.

On August 1, the news broke that Palmeiro—the player who was outraged about being accused of using steroids in the hearing before Congress—tested positive for steroids, specifically the potent anabolic steroid stanazol, and was suspended for 10 games. He at first claimed he had no idea how the steroids entered his body, and then implicated teammate Miguel Tejada in the scandal, claiming the steroid may have entered his body through what he thought was a B_{12} shot from Tejada, who denied any involvement.

Palmeiro issued a statement, but kept a low profile. "I have never intentionally used steroids. Never. Ever. Period," he said. "Ultimately, although I never intentionally put a banned substance into my body, the independent arbitrator ruled that I had to be suspended under the terms of the program," he added in the statement. But few people believed his statement.

He was finished. Palmeiro would return to the Orioles and play a handful of games, but he was vilified by both Orioles fans and people nationwide for his positive test, which had come in the same year he passed the 3,000-hit mark, to go along with his 569 career home runs. Those numbers were believed to make him a lock for the Hall of Fame. Now it appears unlikely he will ever receive such a honor.

So the trio the Orioles had promoted on their media guide— Tejada, Sosa, and Palmeiro—were disgraced or discarded in one form or another before the season ended.

The Orioles finished with a 74–88 record, as if anyone was paying attention by that point. Beattie left the front office, and Flanagan, despite his woeful track record so far, was promoted to executive vice president of baseball operations. Jim Duquette was brought in to be the vice president of baseball operations. Going into 2006, the club was hopeful about some of its younger players, like pitcher Eric Bedard and outfielder Nick Markakis, and the return of second baseman Brian Roberts from the dislocated left-elbow injury he suffered near the end of the 2005 season. There is some hope that under Perlozzo, the direction of the franchise might finally take a turn for the better. The fans of the great baseball city of Baltimore certainly deserve it.

Cal Ripken

A book about the Baltimore Orioles is in many ways a book about Cal Ripken, because his life and times are so intertwined with the history of this franchise.

When he was born in Havre de Grace, about 25 miles north of Baltimore, in 1960, Cal Ripken Jr. was already a Baltimore Oriole. His father, Cal Sr., broke in as catcher for the Orioles in 1957.

His father stayed with the Orioles organization, as a minor league manager in places like Aberdeen, South Dakota; Elmira, New York; and Asheville, North Carolina; and then as coach and briefly manager for the major league club, for a total of 36 years with the organization. Cal Sr. began his career helping to develop such future stars as Davey Johnson and Jim Palmer, and then another generation, including Eddie Murray and Mike Flanagan, and was considered to be the driving force behind the system of playing the game that generally became known as the "Oriole Way."

It has since become more known as the "Ripken Way," as Cal and his brother Billy have built a successful post-career business teaching what their father taught them to a generation of young baseball players, such as the simple motto Cal Sr. taught his sons that would ultimately lead to the defining record of Cal Ripken Jr.'s career.

"If you come to the ballgame, you should want to play," Cal said. "You should want to be in there. It's a team game. Therefore, your teammates count on you and it's the only game that's going on today. So, I don't know...simply put, the way my father always used to tell me, 'If you come to the ballpark, if you can play and you want to play and the manager wants you to play, then you should play.'"

The scoreboard behind Orioles legend Cal Ripken says it all. On September 6, 1995, shortstop Cal Ripken played in his 2,131st consecutive game to break Lou Gehrig's cherished consecutive-games-played streak.

Cal Ripken played. And played. And played so much that one day an entire nation would honor him, and he would help save the game in the process.

Ripken grew up a star athlete at Aberdeen High School and was considered a good young baseball prospect. He had been well-known already throughout the Orioles organization. Many of the players and others, such as manager Earl Weaver, had watched him grow up as a kid, accompanying his father to spring training and the ballpark. The team kept its eye on Ripken Jr.'s progress and exploits.

He was a star at two positions—pitcher and shortstop—and there was sentiment within the Orioles organization that when they drafted him, they should use him as a pitcher. But Weaver had a vision of Ripken being his everyday shortstop and stood his ground, so when Ripken reported to Bluefield for rookie ball in 1978, he would see time in the infield, both at shortstop and third base, and progress quickly until he came up to Baltimore in the latter part of 1981. He played 23 games at third base, and didn't make much of an initial impression, batting just .128 with five hits in 39 at-bats.

Weaver, though, still saw something special, and after the club traded third baseman Doug DeCinces to the California Angels for outfielder Dan Ford, Weaver inserted Ripken as his starting third baseman for Opening Day 1982.

Then, on July 1, with shortstop Mark Belanger at the end of his career, Weaver moved Ripken to shortstop. He had become comfortable at third base—so much so that he had started every game there since May 30. But he would be more comfortable at shortstop, where he would start every game until he slowly began making the move back to third base in 1996.

Ripken would prove why Weaver was so high on him in his first full season. Ripken hit .264 with 28 home runs and 93 RBIs, and was named American League Rookie of the Year. He also began a streak of consecutive innings played that hit 8,243 over 904 games before ending September 14, 1987, when he was eventually taken out of a game by his father, Cal Sr., during his stint managing the Orioles.

In 1983 Ripken emerged as one of the game's biggest stars, batting .318 with 27 home runs and 102 RBIs while leading the league in hits (211), doubles (47), and runs scored (121). He became

By the
NUMBERS

12—The number of Orioles who wore No. 8, (which was retired in 2001 to honor Cal Ripken), including Marvelous Marv Throneberry, the hapless first baseman who played for the Orioles in 1961 and was a symbol for the ineptness of the 1962 Amazin' Mets. Other No. 8s include Andy Etchebarren, Dick Kryhoski, Carl Peterson, Jim Pyburn, Kal Segrist, Bobby Avila, Gene Stephens, Foster Castleman, Tim Nordbrook, and Dave Skaggs.

the first player to win Rookie of the Year and Most Valuable Player in consecutive seasons. He recorded the final putout in the 1983 World Series, a liner off the bat of Garry Maddox, as the Orioles defeated the Phillies in five games for their first World Championship since 1970.

It was the start of what seemed to be a storybook career—a young boy who grew up as part of the Orioles family winding up not only playing for his hometown team, but being its biggest star. And while Ripken was growing up in the Orioles family, they were winning and competing for championships year after year—five pennants and two World Series championships along the way. So when he was part of the third World Series championship, Ripken had no reason to believe the good times would not continue.

But they didn't. The 1983 season marked the end of the Orioles dynasty, as owner Edward Bennett Williams abandoned the player development system and opted to build teams through free agency, resulting in a number of poor decisions that led to the near-demise of the franchise. Over the remaining 18 seasons of Ripken's career, he would play on just seven winning teams, and never make it again to the World Series.

"My first year we went to the last game of the season before we lost to Milwaukee, which was a really exciting season," Ripken said before the start of the 1995 season. "The next year we went on to win the World Series. Looking back on it, I think that maybe I had taken that for granted too much. I was in my second year. I was young and trying to get everything going. All of a sudden you win or you win the World Series. I think that it's been a long time and I've never been back...never been to the playoffs.

TOP 10

Hits Per Season

	Player	Hits	Season
1.	Cal Ripken	211	1983
2.	Cal Ripken	210	1991
3.	B.J. Surhoff	207	1999
4.	Al Bumbry	205	1980
5.	Miguel Tejada	203	2004
6.	Miguel Tejada	199	2005
7.	Cal Ripken	195	1984
8.	Brooks Robinson	194	1964
9.	Roberto Alomar	193	1996
10.	Brooks Robinson	192†	1961
	Brooks Robinson	192†	1962

"I think if I had the opportunity to go back to the playoffs or to the World Series now, I'd be in a position to appreciate it a whole lot more," he said. "When I first came into the big leagues, I thought that after the first two years it was going to be the same throughout the whole career but because it hasn't and because we have lost and because I have endured a rebuilding process I'd love to get back to the World Series and feel that feeling again."

He would come close when the Orioles made it to the League Championship Series in 1996 and 1997, but he would never again play for a World Championship team.

Still, Ripken managed to keep baseball in Baltimore relevant with his talent and determination. At 6'3" and 200 pounds, he redefined the shortstop position. He led the league in assists in 1983, 1984, 1986, and 1987; putouts in 1985; and double plays in 1983 and 1985. He also led all major league shortstops in home runs, RBIs, runs scored, and slugging percentage each year from 1983 to 1986. In 1991, he would win his second MVP award, on a last-place Orioles team, when he hit 34 home runs, drove in 114 runs, batted .323, and had 46 doubles and 210 hits. He would also get a chance to play with his brother, second baseman Billy

Ripken, from 1987 to 1992 and again in 1996, and be managed by his father for a full season in 1987.

Oh, and by the way, he kept playing every game, and with each passing year, the buildup began as Ripken grew closer to what was once perceived as an untouchable record—Lou Gehrig's consecutive-game streak of 2,130 games. On September 6, 1995, the year following the bitter baseball strike that cancelled the postseason and drove fans away from ballparks around the country (and nearly endangered Ripken's record, as Orioles owner Peter Angelos had refused to assemble a replacement team when owners threatened to field such teams for the 1995 season), Ripken brought them back with his magical season when he broke Gehrig's record—something he said he never set out to do.

"I was raised with a work ethic and an approach in baseball or team sports in general, that the object of the team sport is to go out and try to win and help yourself win and do whatever it takes to win," Ripken said. "It's important for you to rely on and count on your teammates to make that all happen...and so, therefore, it was important for me to be counted on by my teammates to be in the lineup every day and so, by working from the premise, I approach each and every game with the fact that I am proud of the streak, for the reasons that my teammates can count on me to be in the lineup and hopefully help do something during the course of the game that is going to help us win. If somebody else can help our team win better than I can, then they should be playing before me. Simply put, I come to the ballpark ready to play, wanting to play, if the manager who's in charge decides he wants to put me in and wants me to play, then I will. That's the way I've always approached it, that's the significance of the streak to me."

The streak would come to an end on September 20, 1998, when Ripken, who had moved to third base permanently in 1997, would go to manager Ray Miller and say it might be best for him to sit out. He was replaced by rookie Ryan Minor. One year later he would be hit hard by the loss of his father, Cal Sr., who died

TRIVIA

How many playoff appearances have the Baltimore Orioles made?

Answers to the trivia questions are on pages 165–166.

from lung cancer. In 2001, Ripken called it quits, and had one final shining moment. He had been voted in at third base for the All-Star Game—his record-setting 19th All-Star Game—but when the AL took the field, starting shortstop Alex Rodriguez, in a plan devised with manager Joe Torre, told Ripken to move to shortstop, where he received a standing ovation and played the game there. He put his signature on the moment with a memorable home run, and was named the game's MVP, his second such award for the contest. The records show he hit 431 career home runs, had 3,184 hits, and drove in 1,695 runs. But the record that will always define Cal Ripken is 2,632—his consecutive-game record, which will likely never be broken.

ANSWERS TO TRIVIA QUESTIONS

Page 5: Bob Turley, who won 14 and lost 15, led the 1954 Orioles in wins.

Page 11: The first Oriole to play in an All-Star Game was George Kell, who started the 1956 All-Star Game at third base.

Page 14: Shortstop Ron Hansen won Rookie of the Year in the American League in 1960.

Page 16: Luis Aparicio and his successor, Mark Belanger, both stole 166 bases in their Baltimore careers. However, Aparicio did it in five seasons, while Belanger did it in 17.

Page 24: Hitting into the most triple plays. Robinson set the record by hitting into the fourth triple play of his career on August 6, 1967, against the Chicago White Sox.

Page 30: Three rookies started for the 1966 Orioles: Davey Johnson at second, Paul Blair in center field, and Andy Etchebarren at catcher.

Page 39: Outfielder Don Buford was known in Japan as the "greatest leadoff man in the world" after the Orioles toured Japan in 1971. He scored 297 runs from 1969 through 1971, and was the most difficult man in baseball history to double-up, grounding in just 33 double plays in 4,553 career at-bats. Buford would later play in Japan, from 1973 to 1976.

Page 40: Seven different Orioles homered in a game against the Red Sox on May 17, 1967: Brooks Robinson, Frank Robinson, Andy Etchebarren, Sam Bowens, Boog Powell, Paul Blair, and Davey Johnson.

Page 51: Mike Cuellar, who went 23–11 in 1969 with a 2.38 ERA, was the first Orioles pitcher to win the Cy Young Award. He shared the honor that year with Denny McLain of the Detroit Tigers.

Page 55: In 1958 Frank Robinson received the Gold Glove, as a left fielder for the Reds.

Page 61: Boog Powell was on the cover of the 1970 Orioles Yearbook.

Page 67: Lee May of the Cincinnati Reds dubbed Brooks Robinson the "Human Vacuum Cleaner" during the 1970 World Series.

Page 74: Pat Dobson, who won 20 games in 1971, was nicknamed "the Snake."

Page 77: In 1970 Dave McNally did something that no other pitcher had ever done—he hit a grand-slam home run in a World Series game.

Page 92: Reggie Jackson hit 27 home runs in his one and only season with the Orioles.

Page 94: Julius Erving was Orioles pitcher Mike Flanagan's basketball teammate at the University of Massachusetts.

Page 97: Ken Singleton won the prestigious Roberto Clemente Award in 1982.

Page 110: The Orioles scored 19 more runs than the Brewers scored in the first three games of the epic four-game Series to close out the 1982 season.

Page 113: Tippy Martinez picked off three straight Blue Jays runners in the tenth inning of an August 24, 1983, game in Baltimore. With the Orioles down 4–3, Martinez picked off Barry Bonnell but then walked Dave Collins. Then he picked off Collins. With two outs, Martinez gave up a single to Willie Upshaw—who Martinez promptly picked off as well, setting a major league record.

Page 116: In 1979 Jimmy Carter was the first president to watch an Orioles game.

Page 118: The Baltimore Orioles were named after a bird that had been named for Lord Baltimore, the founder of Maryland.

Page 122: The Chicago White Sox were the Orioles' Opening Day opponent for the 1991 season opener, the final one at Memorial Stadium. The Sox also opened against the Orioles in 1954.

Page 132: Three broadcasters who spent time with the Orioles have been inducted into the Hall of Fame: Ernie Harwell, Chuck Thompson, and Bob Murphy.

Page 134: Former NBA superstar and future minor league player Michael Jordan participated in the Celebrity Home Run Challenge

at the All-Star Game workout at Camden Yards in 1993. One year later, he would be in a Birmingham Barons uniform playing minor league baseball after shocking the world by retiring from basketball at the end of the 1993 season. His fling with Class AA baseball—and his .202 average—lasted one season.

Page 139: Remarkably, although he drove in more than 100 runs in four straight seasons (from 1982 to 1985), including 124 in the 1985 season, Eddie Murray never won an American League MVP Award. But Murray was voted MVP of the Orioles for five straight seasons—more than any other player in club history—from 1981 to 1985.

Page 142: Roberto Alomar hit the home run that clinched the wild card berth for the Orioles in 1996.

Page 156: June 23 was the last day of the 2005 season that the Orioles were in first place.

Page 163: The Baltimore Orioles have made 10 playoff appearances, including three World Championships and six pennants.

Baltimore Orioles All-Time Roster (through 2006 season)

A

Don Aase (P)	1985–88
Harry Ables (P)	1905
Cal Abrams (OF)	1954–55
Winston Abreu (P)	2006
Bill Abstein (1B)	1910
Jerry Adair (2B)	1958–66
Bobby Adams (3B)	1956
Spencer Adams (2B)	1927
Willie Adams (P)	1912–13
Mike Adamson (P)	1967–69
Sam Agnew (C)	1913–15
Kurt Ainsworth (P)	2003–04
George Aiton (OF)	1912
Ed Albrecht (P)	1949–50
Jay Aldrich (P)	1990
Bob Alexander (P)	1955
Doyle Alexander (P)	1972–76
Manny Alexander (SS)	1992–93, 1995–96
Walt Alexander (C)	1912–13, 1915
Ethan Allen (OF)	1937–38
Johnny Allen (P)	1941
Sled Allen (C)	1910
Mack Allison (P)	1911–13
Mel Almada (OF)	1938–39
Roberto Alomar (2B)	1996–98
Rich Amaral (OF)	1999–2000
Andy Anderson (SS)	1948–49
Brady Anderson (OF)	1988–2001
John Anderson (OF)	1901–03

John Anderson (P)	1960
Mike Anderson (OF)	1978
Ivy Andrews (P)	1934–36
Luis Aparicio (SS)	1963–67
Pete Appleton (P)	1942–45
George Archie (3B)	1941, 1946
Hank Arft (1B)	1948–52
Danny Ardoin (C)	2006
Tony Arnold (P)	1986–87
Elden Auker (P)	1940–42
Jimmy Austin (3B)	1911–29
Bobby Avila (2B)	1959
Benny Ayala (OF)	1979–84

B

Art Bader (OF)	1904
Red Badgro (OF)	1929–30
Ed Baecht (P)	1937
Grover Baichley (P)	1914
Bill Bailey (P)	1907–12
Bob Bailor (OF)	1975–76
Harold Baines (DH)	1993–95, 1997–2000
Floyd Baker (3B)	1943–44
Frank Baker (SS)	1973–74
James Baldwin (P)	2005
John Bale (P)	2000
Mike Balenti (SS)	1913
Jeff Ballard (P)	1987–91
Win Ballou (P)	1926–27

George Bamberger (P)	1959	Frank Bertaina (P)	1964–67, 1969
Steve Barber (P)	1960–67	Fred Besana (P)	1956
Bret Barberie (2B)	1995	Larry Bettencourt (OF)	1928–32
Ray Barker (1B)	1960	Vern Bickford (P)	1954
Red Barkley (2B)	1937	Larry Bigbie (OF)	2001–05
Edgar Barnhart (P)	1924	Pete Bigler	1917
Ed Barnowski (P)	1965–66	Jim Bilbrey (P)	1949
Kevin Bass (OF)	1995	Emil Bildilli (P)	1937–41
Tony Batista (3B)	2001–03	Josh Billings (C)	1919–23
Matt Batts (C)	1951	George Binks (OF)	1948
Rick Bauer (P)	2001–05	Kurt Birkins (P)	2006
Russ Bauers (P)	1950	Babe Birrer (P)	1956
George Baumgardner (P)	1912–16	Frank Biscan (P)	1942–48
Denny Bautista (P)	2004	Rivington Bisland (SS)	1913
Jose Bautista (P)	1988–91	John Black (1B)	1911
Jose Bautista (OF)	2004	George Blaeholder (P)	1925–35
Don Baylor (DH)	1970–75	Paul Blair (OF)	1964–76
Bill Bayne (P)	1919–24	Casey Blake (3B)	2001
Charlie Beamon (P)	1956–58	Sheriff Blake (P)	1937
Gene Bearden (P)	1952	Curt Blefary (OF)	1965–68
Steve Bechler (P)	2002	Bert Blue (C)	1908
Boom-Boom Beck (P)	1924–28	Lu Blue (1B)	1928–30
Rich Becker (OF)	1998	Mike Blyzka (P)	1953–54
Erik Bedard (P)	2002, 2004–06	Mike Boddicker (P)	1980–88
Fred Beene (P)	1968–70	George Boehler (P)	1920–21
Ollie Bejma (2B)	1934–36	Bernie Boland (P)	1921
Mark Belanger (SS)	1965–81	Charlie Bold (1B)	1914
Beau Bell (OF)	1935–39	Stew Bolen (P)	1926–27
Eric Bell (P)	1985–87	Tom Bolton (P)	1994
Juan Bell (2B)	1989–91	George Bone (SS)	1901
Albert Belle (OF)	1999–2000	Ricky Bones (P)	1999
Benny Bengough (C)	1931–32	Julio Bonetti (P)	1937–38
Juan Beniquez (OF)	1986	Juan Bonilla (2B)	1986
Armando Benitez (P)	1994–98	Bobby Bonilla (3B)	1995–96
Fred Bennett (OF)	1928	Luther Bonin (OF)	1913
Herschel Bennett (OF)	1923–27	Bobby Bonner (SS)	1980–83
Joel Bennett (P)	1998	Danny Boone (P)	1990
Kris Benson (P)	2006	Rich Bordi (P)	1986
Johnny Berardino (2B)	1939–47, 1951	Mike Bordick (SS)	1996–2002
Johnny Bero (SS)	1951	Dave Borkowski (P)	2004
Geronimo Berroa (DH)	1997	Joe Borowski (P)	1995
Neil Berry (SS)	1953–54	Babe Borton (1B)	1916

Shawn Boskie (P)	1997	Fritz Buelow (C)	1907
Dave Boswell (P)	1971	Damon Buford (OF)	1993–95
Jim Bottomley (1B)	1936–37	Don Buford (OF)	1968–72
Benny Bowcock (2B)	1903	Al Bumbry (OF)	1972–84
Tim Bowden (OF)	1914	Wally Bunker (P)	1963–68
Brent Bowers (OF)	1996	Chris Burkam	1915
Sam Bowens (OF)	1963–67	Jimmy Burke (3B)	1901
Bob Boyd (1B)	1956–60	Leo Burke (OF)	1958–59
Ray Boyd (P)	1910	Pat Burke (3B)	1924
Gene Brabender (P)	1966–68	Jesse Burkett (OF)	1902–04
George Bradley (OF)	1946	Rick Burleson (SS)	1987
Phil Bradley (OF)	1989–90	Johnny Burnett (SS)	1935
Jackie Brandt (OF)	1960–65	Jack Burns (1B)	1930–36
Otis Brannan (2B)	1928–29	Pete Burnside (P)	1963
Garland Braxton (P)	1931–33	Bill Burwell (P)	1920–21
Lesli Brea (P)	2000–01	Jim Busby (OF)	1957–58, 1960–61
Harry Brecheen (P)	1953	Joe Bush (P)	1925
Marv Breeding (2B)	1960–62	John Butler (C)	1901
Jim Brideweser (SS)	1954, 1957	Kid Butler (2B)	1907
Bunny Brief (1B)	1912–13	John Buzhardt (P)	1967
Nelson Briles (P)	1977–78	Harry Byrd (P)	1955
Chris Britton (P)	2006	Tim Byrdak (P)	2005–06
Chris Brock (P)	2002	Tommy Byrne (P)	1951–52
Herman Bronkie (3B)	1919–22	Eric Byrnes (OF)	2005
Jim Brower (P)	2006	Milt Byrnes (OF)	1943–45
Bill Brown (OF)	1912		
Curly Brown (P)	1911–13	**C**	
Dick Brown (C)	1963–65	Enos Cabell (3B)	1972–74
Elmer Brown (P)	1911–12	Daniel Cabrera (P)	2004–06
Hal Brown (P)	1955–62	Tom Cafego (OF)	1937
Jarvis Brown (OF)	1995	Bob Cain (P)	1952–53
Kevin Brown (P)	1995	Sugar Cain (P)	1935–36
Larry Brown (SS)	1973	Earl Caldwell (P)	1935–37
Lloyd Brown (P)	1933	Bruce Campbell (OF)	1932–34
Mark Brown (P)	1984	Paul Carey (1B)	1993
Marty Brown (3B)	1990	Tom Carey (2B)	1935–37
Walter Brown (P)	1947	Hector Carrasco (P)	2003
Willard Brown (OF)	1947	Chico Carrasquel (SS)	1959
Jack Bruner (P)	1950	Cam Carreon (C)	1966
George Brunet (P)	1963	Joe Carter (OF)	1998
Ed Bruyette (OF)	1901	Raul Casanova (C)	2002
Jim Buchanan (P)	1905	Carlos Casimiro (DH)	2000

George Caster (P)	1941–45	Fritzie Connally (3B)	1985
Foster Castleman (3B)	1958	Joe Connor (C)	1901
Bernie Castro (2B)	2005	Wid Conroy (3B)	1901
Wayne Causey (SS)	1955–57	Sandy Consuegra (P)	1956–57
Art Ceccarelli (P)	1957	Mike Cook (P)	1993
Bob Chakales (P)	1954	Rollin Cook (P)	1915
Harry Chapman (C)	1916	Bob Cooney (P)	1931–32
Norm Charlton (P)	1997–98	Rocky Coppinger (P)	1996–99
Mike Chartak (OF)	1942–44	Doug Corbett (P)	1987
Raul Chavez (C)	2006	Archie Corbin (P)	1996
Bruce Chen (P)	2004–06	Marty Cordova (OF)	2002–03
Tony Chevez (P)	1977	Mark Corey (OF)	1979–81
Tom Chism (1B)	1979	Red Corriden (SS)	1910
Mark Christman (3B)	1939–46	Jim Corsi (P)	1999
Gino Cimoli (OF)	1964	Clint Courtney (C)	1952–54, 1960–61
Al Clancy (3B)	1911	Sam Covington (1B)	1913
Earl Clark (OF)	1934	Bill Cox (P)	1938–40
Howie Clark (OF)	2002, 2006	Billy Cox (3B)	1955
Terry Clark (P)	1995	Doc Crandall (P)	1916
Will Clark (1B)	1999–2000	Jake Crawford (OF)	1952
Nig Clarke (C)	1911	Lou Criger (C)	1909, 1912
Ellis Clary (3B)	1943–45	Dave Criscione (C)	1977
Bob Clemens (OF)	1914	Tony Criscola (OF)	1942–43
Pat Clements (P)	1992	Joe Crisp (C)	1910–11
Verne Clemons (C)	1916	Dode Criss (P)	1908–11
Harlond Clift (3B)	1934–43	Ned Crompton (OF)	1909
Danny Clyburn (OF)	1997–98	Frank Crossin (C)	1912–14
Gil Coan (OF)	1954–55	Bill Crouch (P)	1910
Herb Cobb (P)	1929	Jack Crouch (C)	1930–31, 1933
Ivanon Coffie (3B)	2000	Alvin Crowder (P)	1927–30
Dick Coffman (P)	1928–35	Terry Crowley (DH)	1969–73,
Slick Coffman (P)	1940		1976–82
Rich Coggins (OF)	1972–74	Deivi Cruz (SS)	2003
Ed Cole (P)	1938–39	Todd Cruz (3B)	1983–84
Ed Coleman (OF)	1935–36	Darwin Cubillan (P)	2004
Joe Coleman (P)	1954–55	Mike Cuellar (P)	1969–76
Pat Collins (C)	1919–24	Roy Cullenbine (OF)	1940–42
Ray Coleman (OF)	1947–52	Nick Cullop (P)	1921
Rip Coleman (P)	1959–60	Midre Cummings (OF)	2005
Rip Collins (P)	1929–31	Perry Currin (SS)	1947
Pete Compton (OF)	1911–13	George Curry (P)	1911
Jeff Conine (1B)	1999–2003, 2006	Jack Cust (OF)	2003–04

D

Omar Daal (P)	2003
Angelo Dagres (OF)	1955
Babe Dahlgren (1B)	1942, 1946
John Daley (SS)	1912
Bill Dalrymple (3B)	1915
Clay Dalrymple (C)	1969–71
Dave Danforth (P)	1922–25
Ike Danning (C)	1928
Rich Dauer (2B)	1976–85
Jerry DaVanon (SS)	1971
Butch Davis (OF)	1988–89
Dave Davenport (P)	1916– 19
Dixie Davis (P)	1920–26
Eric Davis (OF)	1996–98
Tommy Davis (C)	1999
Glenn Davis (1B)	1991–93
Harry Davis (1B)	1937
Storm Davis (P)	1982–86, 1992
Tommy Davis (OF)	1972–75
Tommy Davis (C)	1999–2000
Mike DeJean (P)	2004
Delino DeShields (2B)	1998–2001
Charlie Deal (3B)	1916
Dizzy Dean (P)	1947
Paul Dean (P)	1943
Joe Deberry (P)	1920–21
Doug DeCinces (3B)	1973–81
Jim Dedrick (P)	1995
Shorty Dee (SS)	1915
Francisco Dela Rosa (P)	1991
Jim Delahanty (2B)	1907
Luis Deleon (P)	1987
David Dellucci (OF)	1997
Ike Delock (P)	1963
Jim Delsing (OF)	1950–52
Frank Demaree (OF)	1944
Billy Demars (SS)	1950–51
Ray Demmitt (OF)	1910, 1917
Gene Demontreville (2B)	1904
Rick Dempsey (C)	1976–86, 1992
Sam Dente (SS)	1948

John Desilva (P)	1995
Cesar Devarez (C)	1995–96
Mike Devereaux (OF)	1989–94, 1996
Walt Devoy (OF)	1909
Chuck Diering (OF)	1954–56
Gordon Dillard (P)	1988
Bob Dillinger (3B)	1946–49
Bill Dillman (P)	1967
Mike Dimmel (OF)	1977–78
Bill Dinneen (P)	1907–09
Ken Dixon (P)	1984–87
Leo Dixon (C)	1925–27
Pat Dobson (P)	1971–72
Tom Dodd (DH)	1986
Jiggs Donahue (1B)	1901–02
Red Donahue (P)	1902–03
Len Dondero (3B)	1929
Harry Dorish (P)	1950,
	1955–56
Sean Douglass (P)	2001–03
Pete Dowling (P)	1901
Jess Doyle (P)	1931
Doug Drabek (P)	1998
Moe Drabowsky (P)	1966–68,
	1970
Dick Drago (P)	1977
Clem Dreisewerd (P)	1948
Karl Drews (P)	1948–49
Travis Driskill (P)	2002–03
Walt Dropo (1B)	1959–61
Eric DuBose (P)	2002–05
Hugh Duffy (OF)	1901
Jim Duggan (1B)	1911
Tom Dukes (P)	1971
Dave Duncan (C)	1975–76
Ryne Duren (P)	1954
Joe Durham (OF)	1954–57
Cedric Durst (OF)	1922–26
Jim Dwyer (OF)	1981–88
Jim Dyck (OF)	1951–53,
	1955–56
Radhames Dykhoff (P)	1998

E

Jake Early (C)	1947
Carl East (OF)	1915
Hank Edwards (OF)	1953
Mark Eichhorn (P)	1994
George Elder (OF)	1949
Frank Ellerbe (3B)	1921–24
Bob Elliott (3B)	1953
Jumbo Elliott (P)	1923
Verdo Elmore (OF)	1924
Red Embree (P)	1949
Jack Enzenroth (C)	1914
Hal Epps (OF)	1943–44
Mike Epstein (1B)	1966–67
Scott Erickson (P)	1995–2002
Chuck Essegian (OF)	1961
Bobby Estalella (OF)	1941
Chuck Estrada (P)	1960–64
Oscar Estrada (P)	1929
Andy Etchebarren (C)	1962–75
Dwight Evans (OF)	1991
Joe Evans (OF)	1924–25
Roy Evans (P)	1903
Hoot Evers (OF)	1955–56
Homer Ezzell (3B)	1923

F

Brandon Fahey (OF)	2006
Chet Falk (P)	1925–27
Brian Falkenborg (P)	1999
Cliff Fannin (P)	1945–52
Ed Farmer (P)	1977
Sal Fasano (C)	2005
Stan Ferens (P)	1942–46
Chico Fernandez (SS)	1968
Sid Fernandez (P)	1994–95
Don Ferrarese (P)	1955–57
Rick Ferrell (C)	1929–33, 1941–43
Tom Ferrick (P)	1946, 1949–50
Hobe Ferris (2B)	1908–09
Mike Fetters (P)	1999

Mike Figga (C)	1999
Bill Fincher (P)	1916
Tommy Fine (P)	1950
Jim Finigan (3B)	1959
Steve Finley (OF)	1989–90
Lou Finney (OF)	1945–46
Mike Fiore (1B)	1968
Jeff Fiorentino (OF)	2005–06
Carl Fischer (P)	1932
Eddie Fisher (P)	1966–67
Jack Fisher (P)	1959–62
Red Fisher (OF)	1910
Showboat Fisher (OF)	1932
Tom Fisher (P)	1967
Charlie Flanagan (3B)	1913
Mike Flanagan (P)	1975–87, 1991–92
John Flinn (P)	1978–79, 1982
Bobby Floyd (SS)	1968–70
Hank Foiles (C)	1961
P. J. Forbes (2B)	1998
Dan Ford (OF)	1982–85
Dave Ford (P)	1978–81
Brook Fordyce (C)	2000–03
Mike Fornieles (P)	1956–57
Kris Foster (P)	2001
Eddie Foster (3B)	1922–23
Howie Fox (P)	1954
Tito Francona (OF)	1956–57
Joe Frazier (OF)	1956
Roger Freed (OF)	1970
Alejandro Freire (1B)	2005
Jim Fridley (OF)	1954
Bill Friel (2B)	1901–03
Owen Friend (2B)	1949–50
John Frill (P)	1912
Emil Frisk (OF)	1905–07
Todd Frohwirth (P)	1991–93
Charlie Fuchs (P)	1943
Jim Fuller (OF)	1973–74
Chris Fussell (P)	1998

G

Eddie Gaedel	1951
Joe Gaines (OF)	1963–64
Denny Galehouse (P)	1941–47
Dave Gallagher (OF)	1990
Joe Gallagher (OF)	1939–40
Bert Gallia (P)	1918–20
Chico Garcia (2B)	1954
Jesse Garcia (SS)	1999–2000
Karim Garcia (OF)	2000, 2004
Kiko Garcia (SS)	1976–80
Luis C. Garcia (OF)	2002
Billy Gardner (2B)	1956–59
Wayne Garland (P)	1973–76
Debs Garms (OF)	1932–35
Ned Garver (P)	1948–52
Ned Garvin (P)	1901
Tom Gastall (C)	1955–56
Milt Gaston (P)	1925–27
Joe Gedeon (2B)	1918–20
Phil Geier (OF)	1901
Jim Gentile (1B)	1960–63
Lefty George (P)	1911
Wally Gerber (SS)	1917–28
Ken Gerhart (OF)	1986–88
Al Gerheauser (P)	1948
Lou Gertenrich (OF)	1901
Joe Giard (P)	1925–26
Jay Gibbons (OF)	2001–06
Charlie Gibson (C)	1905
Geronimo Gil (C)	2001–05
Billy Gilbert (2B)	1901
George Gill (P)	1939
Paul Gilliford (P)	1967
Jack Gilligan (P)	1909–10
Joe Ginsberg (C)	1956–60
Tony Giuliani (C)	1936–37
Fred Glade (P)	1904–07
Billy Gleason (2B)	1921
Harry Gleason (3B)	1904–05
Joe Glenn (C)	1939
Gordon Goldsberry (1B)	1952

Mike Goliat (2B)	1951–52
Chris Gomez (SS)	2005–06
Leo Gomez (3B)	1990–95
Rene Gonzales (3B)	1987–90
Billy Goodman (2B)	1957
Curtis Goodwin (OF)	1995
Goose Goslin (OF)	1930–32
Claude Gouzzie (2B)	1903
Joe Grace (OF)	1938–46
Mike Grace (P)	2000
Fred Graff (3B)	1913
Bert Graham (1B)	1910
Dan Graham (C)	1980–81
Jack Graham (1B)	1949
Bill Grahame (P)	1908–10
George Grant (P)	1923–25
Dolly Gray (P)	1928–33
Pete Gray (OF)	1945
Ted Gray (P)	1955
Charlie Greene (C)	1997–98
Gene Green (OF)	1960
Lenny Green (OF)	1957–59, 1964
Willie Greene (3B)	1998
Howie Gregory (P)	1911
Bobby Grich (2B)	1970–76
Mike Griffin (P)	1987
Art Griggs (1B)	1909–10
Ed Grimes (3B)	1931–32
Jason Grimsley (P)	2004–05
Ross Grimsley (P)	1974–77, 1982
Bob Groom (P)	1916–17
Buddy Groom (P)	2000–04
Wayne Gross (3B)	1984–85
Johnny Groth (OF)	1953
Frank Grube (C)	1934–35, 1941
Sig Gryska (SS)	1938–39
Ozzie Guillen (SS)	1998
Ted Gullic (OF)	1930–33
Glenn Gulliver (3B)	1982–83
Ernie Gust (1B)	1911
Frankie Gustine (2B)	1950
Jackie Gutierrez (SS)	1986–87

Don Gutteridge (2B)	1942–45	Mike Hart (OF)	1987
Juan Guzman (P)	1998–99	Grover Hartley (C)	1916–17, 1934
		Mike Hartley (P)	1995
H		Paul Hartzell (P)	1980
Bob Habenicht (P)	1953	Roy Hartzell (OF)	1906–10
John Habyan (P)	1985–88	Joe Hassler (SS)	1930
Harvey Haddix (P)	1964–65	Grady Hatton (3B)	1956
Bump Hadley (P)	1932–34	Brad Havens (P)	1985–86
Tom Hafey (3B)	1944	Ed Hawk (P)	1911
Hal Haid (P)	1919	LaTroy Hawkins (P)	2005–06
Jerry Hairston (2B)	1998–2004	Pink Hawley (P)	1901
John Halama (P)	2006	Frankie Hayes (C)	1942–43
Bob Hale (1B)	1955–59	Jimmy Haynes (P)	1995–97
George Hale (C)	1914–18	Ray Hayworth (C)	1942
Sammy Hale (3B)	1930	Red Hayworth (C)	1944–45
Dick Hall (P)	1961–66,	Drungo Hazewood (OF)	1980
	1969–71	Jehosie Heard (P)	1954
Marc Hall (P)	1910	Tommy Heath (C)	1935–38
Ed Hallinan (SS)	1911–12	Jeff Heath (OF)	1946–47
Bill Hallman (OF)	1901	Wally Hebert (P)	1931–33
Earl Hamilton (P)	1911–17	Don Heffner (2B)	1938–43
Jeffrey Hammonds (OF)	1993–98	Emmet Heidrick (OF)	1902–08
Bert Hamric	1958	Mel Held (P)	1956
Larry Haney (C)	1966–68	Woodie Held (SS)	1966–67
Loy Hanning (P)	1939–42	Hank Helf (C)	1946
Snipe Hansen (P)	1935	Rick Helling (P)	2003
Ron Hansen (SS)	1958–62	Ed Hemingway (2B)	1914
Jim Hardin (P)	1967–71	Charlie Hemphill (OF)	1902–07
Pinky Hargrave (C)	1925–26	Rollie Hemsley (C)	1933–37
Larry Harlow (OF)	1975–79	Ellie Hendricks (C)	1968–76, 1978–79
Pete Harnisch (P)	1988–91	Tim Hendryx (OF)	1918
Bill Harper (P)	1911	George Hennessey (P)	1937
Jack Harper (P)	1902	Dutch Henry (P)	1921–22
Tommy Harper (OF)	1976	Pat Hentgen (P)	2001–03
Bob Harris (P)	1939–42	Ramon Hernandez (C)	2006
Gene Harris (P)	1995	Leo Hernandez (3B)	1982–85
Willie Harris (2B)	2001	Ramon Hernandez (C)	2006
Bob Harrison (P)	1955–56	Bobby Herrera (P)	1951
Roric Harrison (P)	1972	Whitey Herzog (OF)	1961–62
Earl Harrist (P)	1952	Johnny Hetki (P)	1952
Sam Harshaney (C)	1937–40	Johnnie Heving (C)	1920
Jack Harshman (P)	1958–59	Kevin Hickey (P)	1989–91

Oral Hildebrand (P)	1937–38	Tim Hulett (3B)	1989–94
Hunter Hill (3B)	1903–04	Bernie Hungling (C)	1930
Billy Hitchcock (3B)	1947	Billy Hunter (SS)	1953–54
Myril Hoag (OF)	1939–41	Dave Huppert (C)	1983
Harry Hoch (P)	1914–15	Jeff Huson (SS)	1995–96
Billy Hoeft (P)	1959–62	Bert Husting (P)	1901
Jim Hoey (P)	2006	Jim Hutto (OF)	1975
Chet Hoff (P)	1915	Dick Hyde (P)	1961
Danny Hoffman (OF)	1908–11	Pat Hynes (OF)	1904
Willie Hogan (OF)	1911–12		
George Hogriever (OF)	1901	**I**	
Chief Hogsett (P)	1936–37	Pete Incaviglia (OF)	1996–97
Bobby Hogue (P)	1951–52	Hooks Iott (P)	1941, 1947
Chris Hoiles (C)	1989–98		
Ken Holcombe (P)	1952	**J**	
Fred Holdsworth (P)	1976–77	Grant Jackson (P)	1971–76
Al Hollingsworth (P)	1942–46	Lou Jackson (OF)	1964
Bobo Holloman (P)	1953	Reggie Jackson (OF)	1976
Darren Holmes (P)	2000	Ron Jackson (1B)	1984
Herm Holshouser (P)	1930	Baby Doll Jacobson (OF)	1915–26
Brian Holton (P)	1989–90	Beany Jacobson (P)	1906–07
Ken Holtzman (P)	1976	Sig Jakucki (P)	1936–45
Don Hood (P)	1973–74	Bill James (P)	1914–15
Paul Hopkins (P)	1929	Ray Jansen (3B)	1910
Sam Horn (DH)	1990–92	Heinie Jantzen (OF)	1912
Rogers Hornsby (2B)	1933–37	Jesse Jefferson (P)	1973–75
Byron Houck (P)	1918	Stan Jefferson (OF)	1989–90
Art Houtteman (P)	1957	Joe Jenkins (C)	1914
Bruce Howard (P)	1968	Tom Jenkins (OF)	1929–32
Ivan Howard (1B)	1914–15	Bill Jennings (SS)	1951
Harry Howell (P)	1904–10	Doug Johns (P)	1998–99
Trenidad Hubbard (OF)	2000	Pete Johns (3B)	1918
Ken Huckaby (C)	2004	Bob Johnson (SS)	1963–67
Rex Hudler (2B)	1986	Charles Johnson (C)	1999–2000
Willis Hudlin (P)	1940, 1944	Chet Johnson (P)	1946
Hal Hudson (P)	1952	Connie Johnson (P)	1956–58
Frank Huelsman (OF)	1904	Darrell Johnson (C)	1952, 1962
Ben Huffman (C)	1937	Dave Johnson (P)	1974–75
Phil Huffman (P)	1985	Dave Johnson (P)	1989–91
Keith Hughes (OF)	1988	Davey Johnson (2B)	1965–72
Roy Hughes (2B)	1938–39	Don Johnson (P)	1950–51, 1955
Mark Huismann (P)	1989	Ernie Johnson (SS)	1916–18

Ernie Johnson (P)	1959	Ron Kittle (OF)	1990
Fred Johnson (P)	1938–39	Billy Klaus (SS)	1959–60
Jason Johnson (P)	1999–2003	Steve Kline (P)	2005
Jim Johnson (P)	2006	Scott Klingenbeck (P)	1994–95
Mike Johnson (P)	1997	Nap Kloza (OF)	1931–32
Johnny Johnston (OF)	1913	Clyde Kluttz (C)	1951
Doug Jones (P)	1995	Bill Knickerbocker (SS)	1937
Earl Jones (P)	1945	Ray Knight (3B)	1987
Gordon Jones (P)	1960–61	Jack Knott (P)	1933–38
Odell Jones (P)	1986	Darold Knowles (P)	1965
Sam Jones (P)	1927	Ben Koehler (OF)	1905–06
Sam Jones (P)	1964	Ryan Kohlmeier (P)	2000–01
Stacy Jones (P)	1991	Dick Kokos (OF)	1948–54
Tom Jones (1B)	1904–09	Ray Kolp (P)	1921–24
		Brad Komminsk (OF)	1990
K		Ernie Koob (P)	1915–19
Mike Kahoe (C)	1902–04	Dave Koslo (P)	1954
Scott Kamieniecki (P)	1998–99	Lou Koupal (P)	1937
Harry Kane (P)	1902	Jack Kramer (P)	1939–47
Dick Kauffman (1B)	1914–15	Mike Kreevich (OF)	1943–45
George Kell (3B)	1956–57	Wayne Krenchicki (3B)	1979–81
Frank Kellert (1B)	1953–54	Red Kress (SS)	1927–32, 1938–39
Pat Kelly (OF)	1977–80	Lou Kretlow (P)	1950, 1953–55
Bill Kennedy (P)	1948–51	Paul Krichell (C)	1911–12
Bob Kennedy (OF)	1954–55	Rick Krivda (P)	1995–97
Ray Kennedy	1916	Dick Kryhoski (1B)	1952–54
Terry Kennedy (C)	1987–88	Ed Kusel (P)	1909
Vern Kennedy (P)	1939–41	Joe Kutina (1B)	1911–12
Bill Kenworthy (2B)	1917	Bob Kuzava (P)	1954–55
Joe Kerrigan (P)	1978–80		
Phil Ketter (C)	1912	**L**	
Jimmy Key (P)	1997–98	Chet Laabs (OF)	1939–46
Paul Kilgus (P)	1991	Lee Lacy (OF)	1985–87
Bill Killefer (C)	1909–10	Joe Lake (P)	1910–12
Harry Kimberlin (P)	1936–39	Tim Laker (C)	1997
Chad Kimsey (P)	1929–32	Al LaMacchia (P)	1943–46
Ellis Kinder (P)	1946–47	Lyman Lamb (3B)	1920–21
Gene Kingsale (OF)	1996, 1998–2001	Bobby Lamotte (SS)	1925–26
Mike Kinkade (OF)	2000–01	Hobie Landrith (C)	1962–63
Mike Kinnunen (P)	1986–87	Tito Landrum (OF)	1983, 1988
Ed Kinsella (P)	1910	Max Lanier (P)	1953
Willie Kirkland (OF)	1964	Frank Laporte (2B)	1911–12

Don Larsen (P)	1953–54, 1965
Lyn Lary (SS)	1935–36, 1940
Bill Lasley (P)	1924
Charlie Lau (C)	1961–67
Doc Lavan (SS)	1913–17
Roxie Lawson (P)	1939–40
Pete Laydon (OF)	1948
Tom Leahy (C)	1901
John Leary (1B)	1914–15
Aaron Ledesma (P)	1997
Billy Lee (OF)	1915–16
Dud Lee (SS)	1920–21
Mark Lee (P)	1995
Craig Lefferts (P)	1992
Jim Lehew (P)	1961–62
Ken Lehman (P)	1957–58
Paul Lehner (OF)	1946–49, 1951
Lefty Leifield (P)	1918–20
Don Lenhardt (OF)	1950–54
Jose Leon (1B)	2002–04
Mark Leonard (OF)	1993
Dave Leonhard (P)	1967–72
Don Leppert (2B)	1955
Walt Leverenz (P)	1913–15
Hod Leverette (P)	1920
Jim Levey (SS)	1930–33
Mark Lewis (2B)	2000
Richie Lewis (P)	1992, 1998
Glenn Liebhardt (P)	1936–38
Kerry Ligtenberg (P)	2003
Fred Link (P)	1910
Ed Linke (P)	1938
Doug Linton (P)	1999
Johnny Lipon (SS)	1953
Nig Lipscomb (2B)	1937
Dick Littlefield (P)	1952–54
Chuck Locke (P)	1955
Whitey Lockman (1B)	1959
Billy Loes (P)	1956–59
Adam Loewen (P)	2006
Sherm Lollar (C)	1949–51
Dale Long (1B)	1951
Ed Lopat (P)	1955
Carlos Lopez (OF)	1978
Javy Lopez (C)	2004–06
Luis Lopez (SS)	2002, 2004
Marcelino Lopez (P)	1967, 1969–70
Rodrigo Lopez (P)	2002–06
Grover Lowdermilk (P)	1915, 1917–19
John Lowenstein (OF)	1979–85
Johnny Lucadello (2B)	1938–46
Steve Luebber (P)	1981
Dick Luebke (P)	1962
Fernando Lunar (C)	2000–02
Don Lund (OF)	1948
Joe Lutz (1B)	1951
Adrian Lynch (P)	1920
Fred Lynn (OF)	1985–88
George Lyons (P)	1924

M

Bob Mabe (P)	1960
Robert Machado (C)	2003–04
Elliott Maddox (OF)	1977
Dave Madison (P)	1952
Calvin Maduro (P)	2000–02
Lee Magee (OF)	1917
Jack Maguire (OF)	1951
Roy Mahaffey (P)	1936
Bob Mahoney (P)	1951–52
John Maine (P)	2004–05
Fritz Maisel (3B)	1918
George Maisel (OF)	1913
Hank Majeski (3B)	1955
Val Majewski (OF)	2004
Alex Malloy (P)	1910
Bob Malloy (P)	1949
Billy Maloney (OF)	1901–02
Frank Mancuso (C)	1944–46
Clyde Manion (C)	1928–30
Ernie Manning (P)	1914
Julio Manon (P)	2006
Jeff Manto (3B)	1995
Heinie Manush (OF)	1928–30

Rolla Mapel (P)	1919	Hank McDonald (P)	1933
Cliff Mapes (OF)	1951	Jim McDonald (P)	1951, 1955
Johnny Marcum (P)	1939	Joe McDonald (3B)	1910
Marty Marion (SS)	1952–53	Roger McDowell (P)	1996
Nick Markakis (OF)	2006	Chuck McElroy (P)	2000–01
Duke Markell (P)	1951	Kevin McGehee (P)	1993
Roger Marquis (OF)	1955	Bill McGill (P)	1907
Eli Marrero (C)	2005	Beauty McGowan (OF)	1928–29
Armando Marsans (OF)	1916–17	Scott McGregor (P)	1976–88
Fred Marsh (3B)	1951–52, 1955–56	Mickey McGuire (SS)	1962–67
Cuddles Marshall (P)	1950	Ryan McGuire (1B)	2002
Jim Marshall (1B)	1958	Archie McKain (P)	1941–43
Babe Martin (OF)	1944–46, 1953	Reeve McKay (P)	1915
Joe Martin (OF)	1903	Jeff McKnight (1B)	1990–91
Morrie Martin (P)	1956	Jim McLaughlin (3B)	1932
Speed Martin (P)	1917	Mark McLemore (2B)	1992–94
Chito Martinez (OF)	1991–93	Marty McManus (2B)	1920–26
Dennis Martinez (P)	1976–86	Norm McMillan (3B)	1924
Tippy Martinez (P)	1976–86	Dave McNally (P)	1962–74
Tom Matchick (SS)	1972	Earl McNeely (OF)	1928–31
Terry Mathews (P)	1996–98	Glenn McQuillen (OF)	1938–47
Luis Matos (OF)	2000–06	George McQuinn (1B)	1938–45
Gary Matthews (OF)	2002–03	Irv Medlinger (P)	1949–51
Charlie Maxwell (OF)	1955	Tommy Mee (SS)	1910
Dave May (OF)	1967–70	Heinie Meine (P)	1922
Derrick May (OF)	1999	Walt Meinert (OF)	1913
Lee May (1B)	1975–80	Sam Mele (OF)	1954
Rudy May (P)	1976–77	Francisco Melendez (1B)	1989
Wally Mayer (C)	1919	Ski Melillo (2B)	1926–35
Mel Mazzera (OF)	1935–39	Paul Meloan (OF)	1911
Bill McAfee (P)	1934	Bob Melvin (C)	1989–91
Jimmy McAleer (OF)	1902–07	Mike Meola (P)	1936
Jack McAleese (OF)	1909	Jose Mercedes (P)	2000–01
Bill McAllester (C)	1913	Luis Mercedes (OF)	1991–93
George McBride (SS)	1901	Kent Mercker (P)	1996
Tim McCabe (P)	1915–18	Jose Mesa (P)	1987, 1990–92
Jerry McCarthy (1B)	1948	Bobby Messenger (OF)	1914
Barry McCormick (3B)	1902–03	Alex Metzler (OF)	1930
Mike McCormick (P)	1963–64	Cass Michaels (2B)	1952
Bill McCorry (P)	1909	Ed Mickelson (1B)	1953
Ben McDonald (P)	1989–95	Eddie Miksis (2B)	1957–58
Darnell McDonald (OF)	2004	Bob Milacki (P)	1988–92

Mike Milchin (P)	1996	Cy Morgan (P)	1903–05, 1907
Kevin Millar (1B)	2006	Mike Morgan (P)	1987–89
Bill Miller (P)	1937	Mike Moriarty (SS)	2002
Bill Miller (P)	1955	Dan Morogiello (P)	1983
Bing Miller (OF)	1926–27	Bugs Morris (P)	1918, 1921
Charlie Miller (SS)	1912	John Morris (P)	1968
Dyar Miller (P)	1975–77	Walter Moser (P)	1911
Ed Miller (1B)	1912–14	Damian Moss (P)	2003
John Miller (P)	1962–67	Les Moss (C)	1946–55
Otto Miller (3B)	1927	Chad Mottola (OF)	2004
Ox Miller (P)	1943, 1945–46	Curt Motton (OF)	1967–71, 1973–74
Randy Miller (P)	1977	Glen Moulder (P)	1947
Stu Miller (P)	1963–67	Allie Moulton (2B)	1911
Ward Miller (OF)	1916–17	Lyle Mouton (OF)	1998
Randy Milligan (1B)	1989–92	Jamie Moyer (P)	1992–95
Alan Mills (P)	1992–98, 2000–01	Heinie Mueller (OF)	1935
Buster Mills (OF)	1938	Billy Mullen (3B)	1920–21, 1928
Lefty Mills (P)	1934–40	Bob Muncrief (P)	1937–47
Al Milnar (P)	1943, 1946	Bobby Munoz (P)	1998
Ryan Minor (3B)	1998–2000	Ed Murray (SS)	1917
Paul Mirabella (P)	1983	Eddie Murray (1B)	1977–88, 1996
Willy Miranda (SS)	1952–53, 1955–59	Jim Murray (OF)	1911
John Mitchell (P)	1990	Ray Murray (C)	1954
Paul Mitchell (P)	1975	Tony Muser (1B)	1975–77
Roy Mitchell (P)	1910–14	Mike Mussina (P)	1991–2000
Bill Mizeur	1923–24	Greg Myers (C)	2000–01
Ron Moeller (P)	1956–58	Hap Myers (1B)	1911
George Mogridge (P)	1925	Jimmy Myers (P)	1996
Gabe Molina (P)	1999–2000	Randy Myers (P)	1996–97
Izzy Molina (C)	2002		
Bob Molinaro (OF)	1979	**N**	
Vince Molyneaux (P)	1917	Buddy Napier (P)	1912
Gene Moore (OF)	1944–45	Al Naples (SS)	1949
Ray Moore (P)	1955–57	Buster Narum (P)	1963
Scrappy Moore (3B)	1917	Bob Neighbors (SS)	1939
Andres Mora (OF)	1976–78	Red Nelson (P)	1910–12
Melvin Mora (3B)	2000–06	Roger Nelson (P)	1968
Jose Morales (DH)	1981–82	Tex Nelson (OF)	1955–57
Willie Morales (C)	2000	Otto Neu (SS)	1917
Charles Moran (SS)	1904–05	Ernie Nevers (P)	1926–28
Jose Morban (SS)	2003	David Newhan (OF)	2004–06
Keith Moreland (OF)	1989	Maury Newlin (P)	1940–41

Patrick Newnam (1B)	1910–11
Bobo Newsom (P)	1934–35, 1938–39, 1943
Carl Nichols (C)	1986–88
Dave Nicholson (OF)	1960–62
Tom Niedenfuer (P)	1987–88
Bob Nieman (OF)	1951–52, 1956–59
Johnny Niggeling (P)	1940–43
Harry Niles (OF)	1906–07
Ramon Nivar (C)	2005
Donell Nixon (OF)	1990
Matt Nokes (C)	1995
Joe Nolan (C)	1982–85
Dickie Noles (P)	1988
Tim Nordbrook (SS)	1974–76
Lou Nordyke (1B)	1906
Hub Northen (OF)	1910
Jim Northrup (OF)	1974–75
Les Nunamaker (C)	1918

O

George O'Brien (C)	1915
Pete O'Brien (2B)	1906
Jack O'Connor (C)	1904–10
Jack O'Connor (P)	1987
Billy O'Dell (P)	1954–59
John O'Donoghue (P)	1968
John O'Donoghue (P)	1993
Charley O'Leary (SS)	1934
Tom O'Malley (3B)	1985–86
Steve O'Neill (C)	1927–28
Frank O'Rourke (3B)	1927–31
Johnny Oates (C)	1970–72
Sherman Obando (OF)	1993, 1995–96
Chuck Oertel (OF)	1958
Jack Ogden (P)	1928–29
Bob Oliver (1B)	1974
Gregg Olson (P)	1988–93
Mike Oquist (P)	1993–95
Jesse Orosco (P)	1995–99
John Orsino (C)	1963–65
Joe Orsulak (OF)	1988–92
Russ Ortiz (P)	2006

Keith Osik (C)	2004
Fritz Ostermueller (P)	1941–43
Joe Ostrowski (P)	1948–50
Willis Otanez (3B)	1998–99
Stubby Overmire (P)	1950–52

P

John Pacella (P)	1984
Dick Padden (2B)	1902–05
Dave Pagan (P)	1976
Mike Pagliarulo (3B)	1993
Satchel Paige (P)	1951–53
Erv Palica (P)	1955–56
Rafael Palmeiro (1B)	1994–98, 2004–05
Jim Palmer (P)	1965–84
Emilio Palmero (P)	1921
John Papa (P)	1961–62
Al Papai (P)	1949
Milt Pappas (P)	1957–65
Al Pardo (C)	1985–86
Mark Parent (C)	1992–93, 1996
Kelly Paris (3B)	1985–86
Jim Park (P)	1915–17
Pat Parker (OF)	1915
Chad Paronto (P)	2001
John Parrish (P)	2000–01, 2003–05
Mike Parrott (P)	1977
Roy Partee (C)	1948
Corey Patterson (OF)	2006
Ham Patterson (1B)	1909
Tom Patton (C)	1957
Gene Paulette (1B)	1916–17
Albie Pearson (OF)	1959–60
Eddie Pellagrini (SS)	1948–49
Barney Pelty (P)	1903–12
Orlando Pena (P)	1971–73
Hayden Penn (P)	2005–06
Brad Pennington (P)	1993–95
Kewpie Pennington (P)	1917
Ray Pepper (OF)	1934–36
Oswaldo Peraza (P)	1988
Yorkis Perez (P)	2002

Scott Perry (P)	1915
Parson Perryman (P)	1915
Rusty Peters (2B)	1947
Buddy Peterson (SS)	1957
Sid Peterson (P)	1943
Jeff Pfeffer (P)	1911
Dave Philley (OF)	1955–56, 1960–61
Tom Phillips (P)	1915
Tom Phoebus (P)	1966–70
Calvin Pickering (DH)	1998–99
Ollie Pickering (OF)	1907
Al Pilarcik (OF)	1957–60
Duane Pillette (P)	1950–55
Lou Piniella (OF)	1964
Jim Pisoni (OF)	1953
Eddie Plank (P)	1916–17
Whitey Platt (OF)	1948–49
Lou Polli (P)	1932
Luis Polonia (OF)	1996
Sidney Ponson (P)	1998–2005
Jim Poole (P)	1991–94
Dave Pope (OF)	1955–56
Jay Porter (C)	1952
Arnie Portocarrero (P)	1958–60
Bob Poser (P)	1935
Nels Potter (P)	1943–48
Boog Powell (1B)	1961–74
Jack Powell (P)	1902–03, 1905–13
John Powers (OF)	1960
Carl Powis (OF)	1957
Del Pratt (2B)	1912–17
Joe Price (P)	1990
Jerry Priddy (2B)	1948–49
Earl Pruess (OF)	1920
Hub Pruett (P)	1922–24
George Puccinelli (OF)	1934
Jim Pyburn (OF)	1955–57
Ewald Pyle (P)	1939–42

Q

Art Quirk (P)	1962
Jamie Quirk (C)	1989

R

Rip Radcliff (OF)	1940–41
Tim Raines (OF)	2001
Tim Raines Jr. (OF)	2001, 2003–04
Aaron Rakers (P)	2004–05
Allan Ramirez (P)	1983
Ribs Raney (P)	1949–50
Earl Rapp (OF)	1951–52
Pat Rapp (P)	2000
Chris Ray (P)	2005–06
Farmer Ray (P)	1910
Floyd Rayford (3B)	1980–82, 1984–87
Jeff Reboulet (2B)	1997–99
Keith Reed (OF)	2005
Steve Reed (P)	2005
Tony Rego (C)	1924–25
Bill Reidy (P)	1901–03
Mike Reinbach (DH)	1974
Alex Remneas (P)	1915
Merv Rettenmund (OF)	1968–73
Al Reyes (P)	1999–2000
Bob Reynolds (P)	1972–75
Carl Reynolds (OF)	1933
Harold Reynolds (2B)	1993
Arthur Rhodes (P)	1991–99
Del Rice (C)	1960
Harry Rice (OF)	1923–27
Scott Rice (P)	2006
Chris Richard (OF)	2000–02
Tom Richardson	1917
Pete Richert (P)	1967–71
Ray Richmond (P)	1920–21
Branch Rickey (C)	1905–06, 1914
Jim Riley (2B)	1921
Matt Riley (P)	1999, 2003–04
Jeff Rineer (P)	1979
Billy Ripken (2B)	1987–92, 1996
Cal Ripken Jr. (SS)	1981–2001
Jim Rivera (OF)	1952
Luis Rivera (P)	2000
Sendy Rleal (P)	2006
Brian Roberts (2B)	2001–06

Robin Roberts (P)	1962–65	Dee Sanders (P)	1945
Willis Roberts (P)	2001–03	Roy Sanders (P)	1920
Charlie Robertson (P)	1926	Fred Sanford (P)	1943–48, 1951
Gene Robertson (3B)	1919–26	Frank Saucier (OF)	1951
Brooks Robinson (3B)	1955–77	Bob Savage (P)	1949
Earl Robinson (OF)	1961–64	Bob Saverine (2B)	1959–64
Eddie Robinson (1B)	1957	Ollie Sax (3B)	1928
Frank Robinson (OF)	1966–71	Steve Scarsone (2B)	1992
Jeff Robinson (P)	1991	Sid Schacht (P)	1950–51
Sergio Robles (C)	1972–73	Art Schallock (P)	1955
Ike Rockenfield (2B)	1905–06	Wally Schang (C)	1926–29
Aurelio Rodriguez (3B)	1983	Art Scharein (3B)	1932–34
Eddy Rodriguez (P)	2004, 2006	John Scheneberg (P)	1920
Nerio Rodriguez (P)	1996–98	Joe Schepner (3B)	1919
Vic Rodriguez (2B)	1984	Bill Scherrer (P)	1988
Gary Roenicke (OF)	1978–85	Curt Schilling (P)	1988–91
Ed Roetz (SS)	1929	Dutch Schliebner (1B)	1923
Ed Rogers (SS)	2002, 2005–06	Ray Schmandt (1B)	1915
Tom Rogers (P)	1917–19	George Schmees (OF)	1952
Saul Rogovin (P)	1955	Dave Schmidt (P)	1987–89
Stan Rojek (SS)	1952	Pete Schmidt (P)	1913
Charlie Root (P)	1923	Johnny Schmitz (P)	1956
Mel Rosario (C)	1997	Hank Schmulbach	1943
Chuck Rose (P)	1909	Jeff Schneider (P)	1981
Claude Rossman (1B)	1909	Rick Schu (3B)	1988–89
Frank Roth (C)	1905	Johnny Schulte (C)	1923, 1932
Dave Rowan (1B)	1911	Fred Schulte (OF)	1927–32
Wade Rowdon (3B)	1988	Len Schulte (3B)	1944–46
Ken Rowe (P)	1964–65	Joe Schultz (C)	1943–48
Willie Royster (C)	1981	Blackie Schwamb (P)	1948
Vic Roznovsky (C)	1966–67	Al Schweitzer (OF)	1908–11
Ken Rudolph (C)	1977	Hal Schwenk (P)	1913
Muddy Ruel (C)	1915, 1933	Mickey Scott (P)	1972–73
William Rumler (C)	1914–17	Ken Sears (C)	1946
B.J. Ryan (P)	1999–2005	Kal Segrist (2B)	1955
		David Segui (1B)	1990–93, 2001–04

S

Chris Sabo (3B)	1994	Hank Severeid (C)	1915–25
Brian Sackinsky (P)	1996	Al Severinsen (P)	1969
Lenn Sakata (2B)	1980–85	Luke Sewell (C)	1942
Chico Salmon (2B)	1969–72	Doc Shanley (SS)	1912
Orlando Sanchez (C)	1984	Owen Shannon (C)	1903

Merv Shea (C)	1933	Roy Smith (P)	1991
Larry Sheets (DH)	1984–89	Syd Smith (C)	1908
John Shelby (OF)	1981–87	Wib Smith (C)	1909
Keith Shepherd (P)	1996	Henry Smoyer (SS)	1912
Barry Shetrone (OF)	1959–62	Charlie Snell (C)	1912
Charlie Shields (P)	1902	Nate Snell (P)	1984–86
Tommy Shields (2B)	1992	Russ Snyder (OF)	1961–67
Tex Shirley (P)	1944–46	Moose Solters (OF)	1935–36, 1939
Urban Shocker (P)	1918–24	Bill Sommers (3B)	1950
Tom Shopay (OF)	1971–77	Sammy Sosa (OF)	2005
Ray Shore (P)	1946–49	Allen Sothoron (P)	1914–21
Bill Short (P)	1962–66	Clyde Southwick (C)	1911
Chick Shorten (OF)	1922	Bob Spade (P)	1910
Burt Shotton (OF)	1909–17	Tully Sparks (P)	1901
John Shovlin (2B)	1919–20	Stan Spence (OF)	1949
Norm Siebern (1B)	1964–65	Hack Spencer (P)	1912
Ed Siever (P)	1903–04	Tubby Spencer (C)	1905–08
Roy Sievers (1B)	1949–53	Paul Speraw (3B)	1920
Eddie Silber (OF)	1937–39	Hal Spindel (C)	1939
Nelson Simmons (OF)	1987	Brad Springer (P)	1925
Syl Simon (3B)	1923–24	Jay Spurgeon (P)	2000
Pete Sims (P)	1915	Don Stanhouse (P)	1978–79, 1982
Chris Singleton (OF)	2002	Pete Stanicek (OF)	1987–88
Ken Singleton (OF)	1975–84	Buck Stanton (OF)	1931
Doug Sisk (P)	1988	Charlie Starr (2B)	1905
George Sisler (1B)	1915–27	Dick Starr (P)	1949–51
Dave Skaggs (C)	1977–80	Herman Starrette (P)	1963–65
Lou Sleater (P)	1950–52, 1958	Ed Stauffer (P)	1925
Tod Sloan (OF)	1913–19	John Stefero (C)	1983–86
Heathcliff Slocumb (P)	1999	Bryan Stephens (P)	1948
Al Smith (OF)	1963	Gene Stephens (OF)	1960–61
Billy Smith (2B)	1977–79	Jim Stephens (C)	1907–12
Dwight Smith (OF)	1994	John Stephens (P)	2002
Earl Smith (OF)	1917–21	Vern Stephens (SS)	1941–47, 1953–55
Ed Smith (P)	1906	Earl Stephenson (P)	1977–78
Hal Smith (C)	1955–56	Garrett Stephenson (P)	1996
Lee Smith (P)	1994	Chuck Stevens (1B)	1941–48
Lonnie Smith (OF)	1993–94	Lefty Stewart (P)	1927–32
Mark Smith (OF)	1994–97	Sammy Stewart (P)	1978–85
Mike Smith (P)	1989–90	Fred Stiely (P)	1929–31
Nate Smith (C)	1962	Rollie Stiles (P)	1930–33
Pete Smith (P)	1998	Royle Stillman (OF)	1975–76

Snuffy Stirnweiss (2B)	1950	Dorn Taylor (P)	1990
Wes Stock (P)	1959–64	Joe Taylor (OF)	1958–59
Tim Stoddard (P)	1978–83	Pete Taylor (P)	1952
Dean Stone (P)	1963	Wiley Taylor (P)	1913–14
Dwight Stone (P)	1913	Miguel Tejada (SS)	2004–06
George Stone (OF)	1905–10	Anthony Telford (P)	1990–91,
Jeff Stone (OF)	1988		1993
Steve Stone (P)	1979–81	Johnny Temple (2B)	1962
Lin Storti (3B)	1930–33	Tom Tennant	1912
George Stovall (1B)	1912–13	Luis Terrero (OF)	2006
Alan Strange (SS)	1934–35,	John Terry (P)	1903
	1940–42	Mickey Tettleton (C)	1988–90
Ed Strelecki (P)	1928–29	Bud Thomas (SS)	1951
Phil Stremmel (P)	1909–10	Fay Thomas (P)	1935
Bill Strickland (P)	1937	Leo Thomas (3B)	1950, 1952
Luke Stuart (2B)	1921	Tommy Thomas (P)	1936–37
Marlin Stuart (P)	1952–54	Valmy Thomas (C)	1960
Guy Sturdy (1B)	1927–28	Frank Thompson (3B)	1920
Jim Suchecki (P)	1951	Hank Thompson (3B)	1947
Willie Sudhoff (P)	1902–05	Tommy Thompson (OF)	1939
Joe Sugden (C)	1902–05	Bobby Thomson (OF)	1960
Billy Sullivan (C)	1938–39	Marv Throneberry (1B)	1961–62
John Sullivan (SS)	1949	Mark Thurmond (P)	1988–89
Gordie Sundin (P)	1956	Sloppy Thurston (P)	1923
Steve Sundra (P)	1942–46	Jay Tibbs (P)	1988–90
B.J. Surhoff (OF)	1996–2000,	Les Tietje (P)	1936–38
	2003–05	Johnny Tillman (P)	1915
George Susce (C)	1940	Mike Timlin (P)	1999–2000
Rick Sutcliffe (P)	1992–93	Jack Tobin (OF)	1916–25
Bill Swaggerty (P)	1983–86	George Tomer	1913
Pinky Swander (OF)	1903–04	Mike Torrez (P)	1975
Bud Swartz (P)	1947	Josh Towers (P)	2001–02
Bob Swift (C)	1940–42	Jim Traber (1B)	1984–89
		Gus Triandos (C)	1955–62
T		Mike Trombley (P)	2000–2001
Jeff Tackett (C)	1991–94	Bill Trotter (P)	1937–42
Vito Tamulis (P)	1938	Dizzy Trout (P)	1957
Tony Tarasco (OF)	1996–97	Virgil Trucks (P)	1953
Willie Tasby (OF)	1958–60	Frank Truesdale (2B)	1910–11
Fernando Tatis (3B)	2006	Bob Turley (P)	1951–54
Jesus Tavarez (OF)	1998	Tom Turner (C)	1944
Ben Taylor (1B)	1951	Shane Turner (3B)	1991

U	
Tom Underwood (P)	1984
Dixie Upright	1953
Tom Upton (SS)	1950–51
V	
Harry Vahrenhorst	1904
Fred Valentine (OF)	1959–63, 1968
Fernando Valenzuela (P)	1993
Russ Van Atta (P)	1935–39
Andy Van Slyke (OF)	1995
Ike Van Zandt (OF)	1905
Elam Vangilder (P)	1919–27
Dave Vangorder (C)	1987
Dave Vineyard (P)	1964
Ozzie Virgil (3B)	1962
Jack Voigt (OF)	1992–95
Ollie Voigt (P)	1924
Joe Vosmik (OF)	1937
W	
Rube Waddell (P)	1908–10
Frank Waddey (OF)	1931
Jake Wade (P)	1939
Kermit Wahl (3B)	1951
Eddie Waitkus (1B)	1954–55
Fred Walden (C)	1912
Irv Waldron (OF)	1901
Ernie Walker (OF)	1913–15
Greg Walker (1B)	1990
Jerry Walker (P)	1957–60
Tilly Walker (OF)	1913–15
Jim Walkup (P)	1934–39
Bobby Wallace (SS)	1902–16
Dee Walsh (OF)	1913–15
Jerome Walton (OF)	1997
Pete Ward (3B)	1962
Buzzy Wares (SS)	1913–14
Hal Warnock (OF)	1935
Carl Warwick (OF)	1965
John Wasdin (P)	2001
Ron Washington (SS)	1987

Eddie Watt (P)	1966–73
Art Weaver (C)	1905
Jim Weaver (P)	1934, 1938
Lenny Webster (C)	1997–99
Bob Weiland (P)	1935
Carl Weilman (P)	1912–20
Don Welchel (P)	1982–83
David Wells (P)	1996
Ed Wells (P)	1933–34
George Werley (P)	1956
Vic Wertz (OF)	1952–54
Lefty West (P)	1944–45
Sam West (OF)	1933–38
Wally Westlake (OF)	1955
Mickey Weston (P)	1989–90
Dutch Wetzel (OF)	1920–21
Bill Whaley (OF)	1923
Fuzz White (OF)	1940
Hal White (P)	1953
John Whitehead (P)	1939–42
Eli Whiteside (C)	2005
Ernie Whitt (C)	1991
Chris Widger (C)	2006
Al Widmar (P)	1948–51
Alan Wiggins (2B)	1985–87
Bill Wight (P)	1955–57
Hoyt Wilhelm (P)	1958–62
Brian Williams (P)	1997
Dallas Williams (OF)	1981
Dick Williams (OF)	1956–58, 1961–62
Earl Williams (C)	1973–74
Gus Williams (OF)	1911–15
Jimmy Williams (2B)	1908–09
Ken Williams (OF)	1918–27
Todd Williams (P)	2004–06
Mark Williamson (P)	1987–94
Joe Willis (P)	1911
Frank Wilson (OF)	1928
Jim Wilson (P)	1948, 1955–56
Hal Wiltse (P)	1928
Ralph Winegarner (P)	1949
Ernie Wingard (P)	1924–27

Jerry Witte (1B)	1946–47	Bobby Young (2B)	1951–55
Ken Wood (OF)	1948–51	Mike Young (OF)	1982–87
Gene Woodling (OF)	1955, 1958–60	Russ Young (C)	1931
Tim Worrell (P)	2000	Walter Young (1B)	2005
Craig Worthington (3B)	1988–91		
Gene Wright (P)	1903–04	**Z**	
Jim Wright (P)	1927–28	Tom Zachary (P)	1926–27
Rasty Wright (P)	1917–23	Al Zarilla (OF)	1943–49, 1952
Tom Wright (OF)	1952	Gregg Zaun (C)	1995–96
		Todd Zeile (3B)	1996
Y		Sam Zoldak (P)	1944–48
Esteban Yan (P)	1996–97	Frank Zupo (C)	1957–61
Joe Yeager (3B)	1907–08	George Zuverink (P)	1955–59

Notes

Welcome to Baltimore

"When I became manager of the Orioles in 1954, we had a president who said he knew nothing about baseball, and he couldn't have made a truer statement. But as the season went along, he thought he was becoming an expert at the game. Before long, he was saying, 'Dykes, do this,' and 'Dykes, do that.' Late in the season, he kept me in the clubhouse almost until game time, giving me instructions. Finally I said, 'If you don't mind, Mr. Miles, it's 10 minutes until game time, and I have to get out on the field.' 'Okay, Dykes,' Miles said. 'Go ahead.' So as I turned to leave, Mr. Miles called out, 'Before you get out there, Dykes, take that grass off the back of your pants.' I answered, 'That's not grass, Mr. Miles. That's mistletoe.'" Jimmy Dykes, *Birds on the Wing: The Story of the Baltimore Orioles,* Garden City, New York; Doubleday and Company, 1967.

The Richards Influence

"The Orioles brought me up at the end of the year. I came to the park [on September 17, 1955] and the third baseman had gotten hurt. Paul Richards just told me I was playing." Brooks Robinson, "Cornerstone at Third Base," *Baltimore Sun* (May 7, 2004).

"Ask anyone from that time who the fastest ever was. They'll tell you Dalkowski. He just had the gift. I've faced Sandy Koufax, and I'll tell you what: he wasn't faster than Steve." Ray Youngdahl, "The Legend of Steve Dalkowski," *Washington Times* (June 4, 2000).

"Best arm I've ever seen. He was a phenomenon. If he ever could have controlled himself, he would have been great." Pat Gillick, "The Legend of Steve Dalkowski," *Washington Times* (June 4, 2000).

Building a Franchise

"In the second inning, a pitch comes in, hits Clint on the top of his cap, and bounces in front of the plate. He turned to the dugout and yelled, 'See, it didn't get by.'" Whitey Herzog, *Birds on the Wing: The Story of the Baltimore Orioles,* Garden City, New York; Doubleday and Company, 1967.

"For whatever reason, Robin Roberts was willing to share with me, and I wanted to learn." Jim Palmer, *Oriole Magic,* Chicago, Ill.; Triumph Books, 2004.

Brooks Robinson

"I figured it represented my best chance to make the major leagues." Brooks Robinson, "Cornerstone at Third Base," *Baltimore Sun* (May 7, 2004).

"I told them I didn't know why I'd been in York all year. Then I went 0 for 19 with 10 strikeouts the rest of the season." Brooks Robinson, "Cornerstone at Third Base," *Baltimore Sun* (May 7, 2004).

"I'm beginning to see Brooks in my sleep. If I dropped this paper plate, he'd pick it up on one hop and throw me out at first." Sparky Anderson, biography on Brooks Robinson, www.baseballlibrary.com.

"I just happened to be in the right spot in that Series. I tell people that I played 23 seasons and I never did have five games in a row like I did in that World Series. As an infielder you can go a week or two and never get a chance to do something spectacular. In this Series, every game I had a chance to do something outstanding defensively and I was hitting well, too. It was a once-in-a-lifetime five-game Series for me and it just happened to be in a World Series." Brooks Robinson, "Cornerstone at Third Base," *Baltimore Sun* (May 7, 2004).

"What we saw in the World Series was spectacular, but we saw that on a daily basis. It would take a .22-caliber rifle aimed in just the right way to get one past him. Brooks worked hard, even though the game came so easily to him. He'd drive in the big run. He was a champion at it. You wanted him up there in the late innings. I'd rather have him up there instead of me." Boog Powell, *The Baltimore Orioles,* Dallas, Texas; Taylor Publishing, 1994.

"I must be the luckiest man in the world. I keep asking, 'How could any one man be so fortunate?' It's more than any one human being could ask for...one of my blessings was to play in Baltimore. I share this day with my adopted hometown, which supported Brooks Robinson on good and bad days. Baltimore, thank you, I love you all." Brooks Robinson, *The Baltimore Orioles,* Dallas, Texas; Taylor Publishing, 1994.

Frank Arrives

"It probably made me more determined than normal, but I always wanted to have a good year. I guess DeWitt's comment may have given me a little extra urge, especially at the start of the season." Frank Robinson, *My Life Is Baseball,* Garden City, New York; Doubleday and Company, 1975.

"I think we just won the pennant." Jim Palmer, *The Baltimore Orioles,* Dallas, Texas; Taylor Publishing, 1994.

"But we had a strong bond from day one. We never had a cross word between us, never an angry word. I respected him and his space and what he had done for that organization and how long he had been there, and he respected my space. We grew to respect each other even more as the years went on, both as persons and players. We never had any problems." Frank Robinson, "Brooks, Orioles Relate No More," *Washington Times* (September 7, 2005).

Brooks Robinson called Frank a "great teammate. He led by the way he played. We saw when he got to our club what a great player he was. We had a ball." Brooks Robinson, "Brooks, Orioles Relate No More," *Washington Times* (September 7, 2005).

"I know they'll be watching me real close and that they expect a lot out of me." Frank Robinson, *My Life Is Baseball,* Garden City, New York; Doubleday and Company, 1975.

"The first pitch he threw me was a fastball down and in, and I swung and knew I hit it good. I rounded the bases like I usually did, no fooling around, and went back to the dugout. The player said, 'That ball went completely out of the ballpark.' I said, 'Bull, get out of here.' I didn't really believe it until I went back to the outfield at the end of the inning and the crowd gave me a standing ovation." Frank Robinson, *My Life Is Baseball,* Garden City, New York; Doubleday and Company, 1975.

"Sit him down." Drabowsky then called the A's bullpen again, asked to speak to Krausse, and said, "You warm, Lew?" Krause recognized the voice on the other end. Mo Drabowsky, "O's Series Hero Was a Prankster, Too," *Baltimore Sun* (June 11, 2006).

"This is Finley. I just got back in town and I saw that story in the paper Friday about the calls you got Friday night. I'd like to hear your version of the episode." Mo Drabowsky, "O's Series Hero Was a Prankster, Too," *Baltimore Sun* (June 11, 2006).

"This is the worst crowd I have ever seen. Looks like we better play with machine guns." Hank Bauer, *Birds on the Wing: The Story of the Baltimore Orioles,* Garden City, New York; Doubleday and Company, 1967.

Bringing a Championship Home

"I was jumping up and down, hoping that would satisfy them and keep them away. But when I tried to regain my feet, I slipped into the deep end. I went down a couple of times and kept yelling for help when I surfaced. My wife was standing by the side of the pool, and she knows I can't swim. She thought I was kidding, and I guess everybody else did too." Frank Robinson, *My Life Is Baseball,* Garden City, New York; Doubleday and Company, 1975.

"I didn't take a deep breath when I first jumped in because I wasn't really sure if Frank was kidding. When I realized he wasn't, I pushed him for a few yards and then resurfaced for air." Andy Etchebarren, *Birds on the Wing: The Story of the Baltimore Orioles,* Garden City, New York; Doubleday and Company, 1967.

"The funny thing is what went through my mind. When Andy lost contact with me, I could see the headlines, 'Robinson Drowns at Team Party.'" Frank Robinson, *My Life Is Baseball,* Garden City, New York; Doubleday and Company, 1975.

"Years ago, when I saw you at a baseball meeting, I knew you were going to help me, and you did. I really want to thank you, and I appreciate everything you've done for us." Jerry Hoffberger, *Birds on the Wing: The Story of the Baltimore Orioles,* Garden City, New York; Doubleday and Company, 1967.

"I honestly didn't think we would get this kind of pitching. If there was a turning point, it was Drabowsky pitching like he did in the first game. He showed the rest of them what to do, and they just went and done it." Hank Bauer, *Birds on the Wing: The Story of the Baltimore Orioles,* Garden City, New York; Doubleday and Company, 1967.

No Miracles
"Joy in Mudville," Ernest Lawrence Thayer, "Casey at the Bat," *San Francisco Examiner* (June 3, 1888).

Frank Robinson
"Robinson is not a young 30. If he had been 26, we might not have traded him." Bill DeWitt Sr., "Top 25 Athletes of the East Bay," *Contra Costa Times* (June 25, 2006).

"He never played like someone with a chip on his shoulder, although he had a right to feel disrespected. Instead, he took it as a challenge to make [the Reds] regret losing him. In a big way, they did us a favor." Brooks Robinson, "Top 25 Athletes of the East Bay: No. 2, Frank Robinson," *Contra Costa Times* (June 25, 2006).

"There was never any doubt in my mind we would beat them. I think it just proves that if you're dedicated to a cause, if you want something badly enough, you can really do it." Frank Robinson, *My Life Is Baseball,* Garden City, New York; Doubleday and Company, 1975.

"He taught us how to win." Davey Johnson, *My Life Is Baseball,* Garden City, New York; Doubleday and Company, 1975.

"I'm scared to death giving up Frank." Earl Weaver, *My Life Is Baseball,* Garden City, New York; Doubleday and Company, 1975.

"You think you were an important part of the club. You contributed a lot to them. Then suddenly you feel like they think they don't need you anymore. They've got somebody better to take your place. Your feelings are hurt, your pride is hurt." Frank Robinson, *My Life Is Baseball,* Garden City, New York; Doubleday and Company, 1975.

"I'm the first black manager only because I was born black." Frank Robinson, "Top 25 Athletes of the East Bay: No. 2, Frank Robinson," *Contra Costa Times* (June 25, 2006).

Taking Care of Business
"I think this ballclub is probably the best ballclub I've ever been on. I think I made that statement last year and really it is probably more accurate this year than it was last year, because our bench is a little stronger and for all-around, a 25-guy unit, this is the best I have ever

seen." Billy Hunter, *The Baltimore Orioles*, Dallas, Texas; Taylor Publishing, 1994.

Pedal to the Metal

"We were reflecting on 1969 all this year, although no one would come out and say it. We dedicated ourselves since spring training to win the American League championship this year and come out on top in the World Series." Frank Robinson, *My Life Is Baseball*, Garden City, New York; Doubleday and Company, 1975.

"I tell you, getting Frank Robinson in 1966 really put us over the top. We were a good ballclub, and that made us the best around for a while." Brooks Robinson, "Brooks, Orioles Relate No More," *Washington Times* (September 7, 2005).

"Man, that guy is like a human vacuum cleaner down there." Lee May, *The Baltimore Orioles*, Dallas, Texas; Taylor Publishing, 1994.

The Final Run

"I had more team success in Baltimore and became more recognizable playing with the Orioles instead of the Reds. We won two world championships and four American League championships. It was about team success, not individual." Frank Robinson, "Brooks, Orioles Relate No More," *Washington Times* (September 7, 2005).

Life without Frank

"When I played for the Orioles, Earl Weaver only spoke to me twice. Once, our catcher got hurt and I said, 'I'll get in there for you, Earl.' He said, 'Fat chance.' After I got traded, he said, 'Enjoy Atlanta.'" Johnny Oates, www.baseballlibrary.com

Earl Weaver

"On my tombstone just write: 'The sorest loser that ever lived.'" Earl Weaver, *The Quotable Coach*, Franklin Lake, N.J.; Career Press, 2002.

Dalton described Weaver as "a winner." Harry Dalton, *The Baltimore Orioles*, Dallas, Texas; Taylor Publishing, 1994.

Weaver told writers that he would "rather lose making a move" than doing nothing. Earl Weaver, *The Baltimore Orioles*, Dallas, Texas; Taylor Publishing, 1994.

"Everything broke down. The 0 for 4's, the left on bases, the pitchers allowing all those home runs. It just added up." Earl Weaver, *The Baltimore Orioles,* Dallas, Texas; Taylor Publishing, 1994.

A New Era Begins

"Brooks never asked anyone to name a candy bar after him. In Baltimore, people named their children after him." Thom Loverro, *Oriole Magic,* Chicago, Ill.; Triumph Books, 2004.

"We always talked about the 'Oriole Way.' Cal Ripken Sr. was the one who indoctrinated every one of us who came in." Thom Loverro, *Oriole Magic,* Chicago, Ill.; Triumph Books, 2004.

Coming Up Short

Baltimore was a club that didn't "have any weaknesses, as far as I can see. They score runs, and they don't allow very many." Thom Loverro, *Oriole Magic,* Chicago, Ill.; Triumph Books, 2004.

"We knew we had blown that series. A lot of things went against us in those three games. We hit some balls really good, but the Pirates turned double plays on balls that should have been base hits. We didn't get any breaks, and they got the momentum. They were a high-intensity ballclub, and we just couldn't get anything going." Thom Loverro, *Oriole Magic,* Chicago, Ill.; Triumph Books, 2004.

"In that last game, we had our ace going, Palmer, and I thought we were going to win it." Thom Loverro, *Oriole Magic,* Chicago, Ill.; Triumph Books, 2004.

"That was a sad day, and it was doubly disappointing because it was Earl's last game." Thom Loverro, *Oriole Magic,* Chicago, Ill.; Triumph Books, 2004.

Trying Times

"My situation was that I had four Cy Young winners ahead of me in Baltimore. I figured if I kept pitching well down in the minors, sooner or later I would become a minor league free agent and somebody would want me. I figured I could bide my time as long as I could pitch well." Thom Loverro, *Oriole Magic,* Chicago, Ill.; Triumph Books, 2004.

"Don't give up your apartment in Rochester," Peters told Boddicker. "As soon as Palmer is back, you're going down again." Thom Loverro, *Oriole Magic,* Chicago, Ill.; Triumph Books, 2004.

Oriole Magic
"Everybody contributed on that team. Everybody knew their role and what they were supposed to do." Thom Loverro, *Oriole Magic,* Chicago, Ill.; Triumph Books, 2004.

"We were in an elevator together. His father said, 'You're Dan Ford, the guy that broke up my son's no-hitter.' Yup, I'm the one." Thom Loverro, *Oriole Magic,* Chicago, Ill.; Triumph Books, 2004.

"I told him that I couldn't do the same thing that Earl did with him. I didn't want to fight with him, and when I hear something negative coming out of your mouth, you're coming out of the game. He could pitch four or five innings for you, pitch no-hit ball, and come in and say that his arm is stiff. What happens is you send him out the next inning, and he gets crushed. So he tells the press, 'I told Altobelli that my arm was stiffening up,' and they would all come running to me." Thom Loverro, *Oriole Magic,* Chicago, Ill.; Triumph Books, 2004.

"The biggest move we made was when we got Todd Cruz from Seattle." Thom Loverro, *Oriole Magic,* Chicago, Ill.; Triumph Books, 2004.

"It was a blessing in disguise. When he came back, he picked up right where he left off." Thom Loverro, *Oriole Magic,* Chicago, Ill.; Triumph Books, 2004.

Losing the Oriole Way
"We thought coming back in 1984 that we would win it again. But the Tigers got off to that great start and all of a sudden, instead of going out there and playing like we were in 1983, we were chasing and chasing right out of the box, and we always got off to bad starts in April." Thom Loverro, *Oriole Magic,* Chicago, Ill.; Triumph Books, 2004.

"I was fired through the grapevine, which I didn't like at all." Thom Loverro, *Oriole Magic,* Chicago, Ill.; Triumph Books, 2004.

"Somebody was talking to Williams. I don't know who." Thom Loverro, *Oriole Magic,* Chicago, Ill.; Triumph Books, 2004.

"Everything broke down. The 0 for 4's, the left-on-bases, the pitchers allowing all those home runs. It just added up." Earl Weaver, *The Baltimore Orioles,* Dallas, Texas; Taylor Publishing, 1994.

"They're all my sons, all 25 players, and I'll treat them the same." Cal Ripken Sr., *The Baltimore Orioles,* Dallas, Texas; Taylor Publishing, 1994.

Camden Yards

"He [Sutcliffe] told his agent that we were taking advantage of them, that they couldn't say no after seeing this place. That was his reaction to the beauty of Camden Yards." Thom Loverro, *Home of the Game,* Dallas, Texas; Taylor Publishing, 1999.

"Camden Yards has changed the thinking of stadium construction. The thinking now is how can we benefit the city?" Thom Loverro, *Home of the Game,* Dallas, Texas; Taylor Publishing, 1999.

"We just ripped one piece of it up after another. We said, 'We don't want this, we don't want that.' One of the architects said, 'Larry, do you have any idea how much these models cost?' I said, 'No, but we're trying to make a point here.'" Thom Loverro, *Home of the Game,* Dallas, Texas; Taylor Publishing, 1999.

"I was worried that when we went to Camden Yards, we would lose the old Orioles history, the feeling of playing in a place that was special for baseball. But when we got on the field at Camden Yards and started playing there, it seemed like it was a place where baseball had been played before. Intellectually, you knew it was brand new and no baseball had been played there until we got there. But when you walked into the place it was a ballpark. It represented so many things and brought up some deep feelings about the game." Thom Loverro, *Home of the Game,* Dallas, Texas; Taylor Publishing, 1999.

All-Stars and Angelos

"I don't have to apologize to anybody. Anyway, I'm used to being criticized. It happens all the time in Toronto." Thom Loverro, *Home of the Game,* Dallas, Texas; Taylor Publishing, 1999.

"Why you can't get Mike Mussina in a 9–3 game is beyond me. I don't care what your explanation is. If you say you have to save him

for extra innings, you don't have any faith in Duane Ward." Thom
Loverro, *Home of the Game,* Dallas, Texas; Taylor Publishing, 1999.

Eddie Murray

"When you come out of the minors and get into a major league
uniform and all of a sudden hear that, it's awesome. It made me
uncomfortable. But I learned to deal with it, so I could go out and do
my job." Eddie Murray, "As Pain Relents, Murray Reflects," *Baltimore
Sun,* January 17, 2003.

"There were some things that were done that were awful and
rotten. I couldn't win that fight. It's not a level playing field. You can't
pretend that it is." Eddie Murray, "As Pain Relents, Murray Reflects,"
Baltimore Sun, January 17, 2003.

Murray devoted part of his speech to Ted Williams who, during
his Hall of Fame induction in 1966, had said, "I must have earned
this. I know I didn't win it with my friendship with the writers. In
that way," Murray said, "I'm proud to be in his company." Eddie
Murray, "Murray Lets Down the Wall at Hall," www.MLB.com, July
27, 2003.

"To me, words focused on the individual. It had nothing to do
with how you hit or how you played the game. Baseball is a team
game. It's not an *I* or a *me* thing. That's what I learned. And that's
what I still believe in." Eddie Murray, "Murray Lets Down the Wall at
Hall," www.MLB.com, July 27, 2003.

Davey Comes Home

"He was a heck of a pitcher and the sort of teammate that would
make everybody better. When you take two teams that were pretty
equally matched, and at the time the Orioles and the Yankees were,
and take a player like that from one team and put him on another, it
would have had a significant impact. Everything took off for the
Yankees after 1996." Jim Palmer, "Don't Blame Maier," *Washington
Times* (June 3, 2005).

"It was like it was almost spoken into existence." Thom Loverro,
Home of the Game, Dallas, Texas; Taylor Publishing, 1999.

The Fall from Grace

"Three years from now, somebody is going to look pretty smart up here." Syd Thrift, "Orioles Conduct Fire Sale," *Washington Times* (July 29, 2000).

"Cal became the symbol for the American work ethic and the symbol for the American working man." Bud Selig, "Final Salute to Ripken," *Baltimore Sun* (October 7, 2001).

"The kind of man every father would like his son to grow up to be." Bill Clinton, "Final Salute to Ripken," *Baltimore Sun* (October. 7, 2001).

Steroids and Shame, but Home Remains

"I gave Chicago everything that I have. It was a beautiful experience for my wife and family. I had a great time in Chicago, but you have to move on. This is my new house, and I love it." Sammy Sosa, "Sosa Heads to O's," Associated Press (February 4, 2005).

"I have never intentionally used steroids. Never. Ever. Period. Ultimately, although I never intentionally put a banned substance into my body, the independent arbitrator ruled that I had to be suspended under the terms of the program." Rafael Palmeiro, statement issued on August 2, 2005.

Cal Ripken

"If you come to the ballgame, you should want to play. You should want to be in there. It's a team game. Therefore, your teammates count on you and it's the only game that's going on today. So, I don't know...simply put, the way my father always used to tell me, 'If you come to the ballpark, if you can play and you want to play, and the manager wants you to play, then you should play.'" Cal Ripken Jr., transcript, Ripken media session, April 6, 1995.

"My first year we went to the last game of the season before we lost to Milwaukee, which was a really exciting season. The next year we went on to win the World Series. Looking back on it, I think that maybe I had taken that for granted too much. I was in my second year. I was young and trying to get everything going. All of a sudden you win or you win the World Series. I think that it's been a long time and I've never been back...never been to the playoffs.

"I think if I had the opportunity to go back to the playoffs or to the World Series now, I'd be in a position to appreciate it a whole lot more. When I first came into the big leagues, I thought that after the first two years it was going to be the same throughout the whole career but because it hasn't and because we have lost and because I have endured a rebuilding process I'd love to get back to the World Series and feel that feeling again." Cal Ripken Jr., transcript, Ripken media session, April 6, 1995.

"I was raised with a work ethic and an approach in baseball or team sports in general, that the object of the team sport is to go out and try to win and help yourself win and do whatever it takes to win. It's important for you to rely on and count on your teammates to make that all happen...and so, therefore, it was important for me to be counted on by my teammates to be in the lineup every day and so, by working from the premise I approach each and every game with the fact that I am proud of the streak, for the reasons that my teammates can count on me to be in the lineup and hopefully help do something during the course of the game that is going to help us win. If somebody else can help our team win better than I can, then they should be playing before me. Simply put, I come to the ballpark ready to play, wanting to play; if the manager who's in charge decides he wants to put me in and wants me to play, then I will. That's the way I've always approached it, that's the significance of the streak to me." Cal Ripken Jr., *The Only Way I Know,* New York; Viking, 1997.